MW01603176

LOVE LIVES IN A SMILE

(And Other Lawn Mower Lessons)
By Joe Trionfero

ISBN: 979-8-218-87616-6
First Edition, 2025

Cover design: Roger Beck
Printed in Oswego, New York, USA
by Mitchell's Speedway Press

For permissions or correspondence, contact:
jtrionfero@aol.com

This Book is Dedicated to

My Dad, Joseph J. Trionfero. Anyone who reads this book will find my dad's fingerprints all over every aspect of my life. Any good in my life, which I have done, was either with him, for him, or because of him. He was the greatest man I have ever known. There are those who say: "The cup is half empty," and there are those that say: "The cup is half full." My Dad was so positive and grateful, he would simply say: "My cup runneth over."

His Wife, Inez Trionfero. Our mom raised her four kids showing so much love and compassion. Just as important she taught us how to show it to others. It wasn't always easy being married to a man whose mantra was, "Envy the working man." Dad may have been the provider but, it was Mom who did everything for us and there were many times she did alone. She was the rock of our family.

His Kids, Marshall, Ken and Rosanne (my siblings). Who were lucky enough to share in his thirst of knowledge, his search for goodness and his continual outpouring of love. We have been blessed to have had each other following that trail he left for us. And, thank God for Fred, Jeanne, Debbie and Denise and all those years of "Tuesday Night Dinners."

His Grandkids and Great-Grandkids. I urge you to learn and remember everything you can about him. He was always so proud of, and hopeful for you, "The next generation."

Acknowledgements

First of all, I want to thank my wife (and best friend), Denise, for allowing me to pursue yet another dream. She has always supported my unusual and demanding career. Being married to an entertainer has never been easy. My partner in life has even put up with my new obsession of writing these stories down. The woman is so patient and tolerant of every crazy thing I do. Without her, this book would have never been written; more important, this amazing life story would have never flourished. As Harry Chapin once sang: "She's the only story of my life."

Thank you to our five kids, Shawn, Nicole, Kate, Dacey and Jillian for continuing your Grampa's legacy of hard work, love and smiles.

I want to thank four very special people, my brother Marshall Trionfero, my first cousin Anthony DiGaetano, Paul Vandish and Tom Price. I am so appreciative of these good men for a lifetime of friendship, support and influence.

It's also important to mention this book would have never happened, unless Terry Schaffer, Linda Furniss, Karen Decaire, Linda Loomis, Becky Trenca O'Kane (and her brother Larry) showed me, in the very beginning, it was okay to jump in the deep end. Their confidence in me surprised and inspired me.

Thanks to Norm Beck for being our family's artist and his nephew Roger Beck for putting his magic touch on this book. I may have written the book but it was Roger and Mitchell's Speedway Press who built it. Thank You. Thank You. Thank You.

Lastly, I want to thank my good friend S. James Farfaglia, who took me under his wing and spent countless hours guiding, helping and coaching me in writing my stories. Thanks Jim.

A Special Thanks to
My Dad and
My wife
Denise

A heartfelt thank you goes out to my dad for making me a good person and to my wife, Denise, for keeping me one.

4

The Lawn Mower Lessons
(Book Sections)

"Family is Everything"
Herrick Street, Fifth Street, Scriba and Norwich.

"Love Lives in a Smile"
*His smiley faces would always remind us
to be happy and that he loved us.*

"Envy the Working Man"
*"I'm not afraid of dying, I'm only afraid of the day
I can't work." Work is therapy!*

"Have a Thirst for Knowledge"
*The only question that ever really mattered was,
"Did you learn anything?"*

"God, I Love It"
*Revel in the good stuff and be appreciative.
"Thank You. Thank You. Thank You."*

"Top Shelf"
*Although not one of his lessons,
this was one of our dad's favorite sayings.*

"Don't Get Old"
*"Old age is creeping in." Fight it off.
Use all your strength. Don't give it away.*

"Under the Grapevine"
In Heaven, we'll all be together again, and forever.

5

Introduction

On November 20, 2024, I wrote my first story. At my brother Marshall's urging, and with the blessing of Linda Furniss, I posted my first short story. It was an article about my very first band with Linda's late husband, Ray Furniss and Tommy Navagh. I had no idea that there would be such an interest in it. I certainly did not know that it would be the first of 100 stories that I would write.

My only goal was to write positive stories, sharing a much-needed light in a darkening world. I also wanted to leave a record behind for my grandkids, as they got older, to learn more about my life and the lessons I've learned. The more I wrote, the more I realized that most of the stories of my life were connected by a common thread of the lessons I learned from my dad. They were lessons, many of which were, painted on the side of his lawn mower. (Yes, his lawn mower.)

People did read my stories and many began to encourage me to write more. Some even suggested I write a book. I thought they were crazy. At first, I brushed it off as people being kind, but it was a comment I got from a new friend, Karen Decaire, that made me stop and think. In one of her "comments" she said I was a great writer. I responded quickly with I didn't consider myself a writer at all. I told Karen, "I was just a storyteller with some stories burning a hole in the bottom of my heart." She came back with, "I think that's the very definition of a writer." I stopped and thought about that and began to write. I am not trained in the art; I did poorly in Miss Perry's English class, at Kingsford Park School, and I barely got out of Mr Familo's class in HS with a 65 average.

What I really am is a talker. I have been entertaining for fifty years and a motivational speaker in schools for the past 35 years. It's when I heard some positive encouragement from Ms. Linda Loomis, a professional writer and former professor at SUNY Oswego, that I became highly motivated and got serious about writing my stories down. Linda's support, through her comments, propelled me forward and somehow made those stories, that had been laying dormant in my heart for decades, explode onto the page with a passion.

I truly love writing, but what really astounds me is that so many people really wanted to read/hear my stories. So many of you, in my hometown of Oswego, have responded and commented about my life on those pages. I am truly humbled. I have been telling my stories my whole life to anyone that would listen. Unfortunately for my wife, five kids and eleven grandkids, they have been a captive audience and had to listen to my stories for years. So, they do thank you for taking over.

The greatest treasure I have uncovered, during this new endeavor, is the people that I have met along the way who have responded with kindness and interest in my stories and insights. I have made so many new friends and rediscovered so many old friends that I had lost touch with, over the years and because of the miles.

And finally….. the answer is, YES. The question, is one our dad would always ask of us whenever we made a mistake: "Did you learn anything?" Yes, I did Dad. Most of it is in this book. ☺

"My life has been a poor attempt
To imitate the man
I'm just a living legacy
To the leader of the band"

Dan Fogelberg
(EMI April Music Inc.)

"Family is Everything"
(Norwich, Scriba and 36 Herrick Street)

Growing up, the Trionfero kids believed the Italian translation for family was Norwich. Those words were interchangeable. "Norwich" was not only painted on the side of our dad's lawn mower, it was literally carved into the walls of his home. This stemmed from his love of his older half-brother George that lived in Norwich, New York. Dad also adored his two sisters Frances (DiGaetano) and Rose (Ruggio). Both being older, they kind of raised him and their closeness continued throughout their entire lives. These stories reflect the joy I had growing up during that special time with my beloved family of Fifth Street Road. It also shows our closeness remains to this day. Lastly these stories pay tribute to my other families of Norwich, Scriba and, of course, 36 Herrick Street.

11

Lawn Mower Lessons

This past Spring, from our freshly opened window, I heard the first lawn mower of the season in our neighborhood. Just like every other spring, it brought my dad to mind. You see, after God and family, what our dad loved most was his lawn mowers. So, it would only be natural that if he wanted to convey an important message to his kids, he would use that "vehicle" to teach his most valuable life lessons. Every lawn mower our dad ever bought, it's first stop, before bringing it home, was to our "family painting expert," Norm Beck. Then, just like a NASCAR race car Norm would, "trick it out" to our father's precise specifications. The mowers would always be painted with his favorite sayings about life, including work, learning and love.

"Envy the working man." My dad loved to work. He worked long into his eighties and he cherished every minute of it. For as long as his four kids could remember, he would say, "I'm not afraid of dying, I'm only afraid of the day I can't work." He would often remind us, especially in times of trial and tribulations, that "work was therapy." When we were growing up, he worked long shifts, many doubles and sometimes multiple jobs at once supporting his family. He once told of working at the railroad yard while in high school. He and two of his buddies would work the overnight shift at the railroad yard working on a

12

refrigeration car. That all-night shift would consist of a three-man team. One kid shoveling snow into the car, one holding a light and the other, standing inside shoveling (throwing) the snow up into the opening at the top of the car's interior walls into a thin partition. He would say: "It was a little hard as the snow would often fall back into our face or down our shirt but he said, "It was okay, as we would take turns at that job."

"Thirst For Knowledge." My father loved to learn. As a small child, I remember our dad "tinkering" on his workbench in the garage. He would do many of his own home repairs and if there were no projects, he would take things apart and reassemble them, just to see how they worked. Learning, for him, was a lifelong experience that he tried to instill in his children. As kids, when we did something stupid, he wouldn't punish us; instead, he would simply ask, "Did you learn anything?" In his sixties, after losing his long-time job, he came to work for JTS Music, our family business. It was, yet, another opportunity for him to learn more. He would listen to, and label, thousands of songs. I am sure he was the only man his age that knew the lyrics to AC/DC songs. On weekends, he worked as a Deejay and on weekdays he taught himself to repair the sound equipment by trail and error and, of course, taking things apart. He never stopped learning.

"Love Lives in a Smile." Our dad's mantra became our Trionfero family motto. It would be proudly displayed in the biggest letters on all his lawn mowers. Those weren't just empty words, dad lived them. He was aways happy, content and helping others. Mowing lawns was one of his favorite ways to show his love for people. I remember as a kid, him stopping at my Aunt Fran's and Aunt Rosie's house to either mow their lawns or fix their machines.

He would load his riding mower into his blue JTS Van to drive to Baldwinsville to cut my grass. My neighbors would often tease me about it. I laugh to myself when I think back on how proud he was of the little mowing business he built. It was no wonder as he would show up in that blue van, with his own mower, and cut any size lawn in Oswego, NY for $5.00. When I told him he should charge a lot more, he responded with a smile and said, "I just like helping people."

Dad loved his family, friends and neighbors and he showed it. He also loved his lawn mowers. He eventually started buying hand mowers for his kids, have Norm Beck paint them, and then deliver them to our houses. Perhaps his greatest show of love, of all, would be during our family picnics when he would pull out his mower to give his great-grandkids rides in the wagon he would pull behind it.

Looking back now, I wonder if his real motive was just making sure all of his family could see the messages written on the side of that machine. Sayings that mattered to our dad and words that he lived by.

Dad and I Broke into a Church

On July 16 2020, during the "Covid summer," my dad and I broke into the closed (and locked) St Joseph's Church. It was his fault, but my idea. What turned out to be his last outing with me started as I was driving him around to visit all his favorite memories, "haunts."

As we drove down West 1st Street (toward the lake) we were driving by his old church. He began to tell me one of his favorite stories of how "during the war, St. Joe's was full, standing room only, every Sunday." I knew the story by heart, but as I listened attentively, it was good that I did, as he threw me a curve ball. He said, "I'd love to see it again."

He rarely sounded sad and never asked for anything, so let's just say we found an open door. We were totally alone in the cathedral of his youth. He was in awe as he stood in the aisle of his family's church in front of its sacred altar.

St. Joseph's Church and all of its families were very near the core of the Trionfero family history. All of our baptisms, First Communions, Confirmations, weddings and funerals (and some bingo games) happened in that glorious structure that now sits dormant.

As we entered the silent church a thought occurred to me. It was a recent comment from a new friend, Jamie Jo Cooney who said, "I remember you and your family when I was a young girl. Your family used to sit a couple of pews in front of us in church every single Sunday."

The epiphany happened. I thought so many of the good things that ever happened to our Trionfero family had their origin in that church. One of my earliest memories is sitting in "our spot." Every family had, "their spots." Our dad was always sitting between me and my older brother Marshall. Marsh was always causing trouble. (Ok, it was me.)

That church, those masses and those families we shared it with were simply heavenly. Even though I haven't seen most of those people in decades, they will forever remain members of my "St Joe's Family" in my heart.

It was better times for sure. Every Sunday, we gathered between West 1st and 2nd streets to profess our faith, say we were sorry, promise to do better and perhaps enjoy coffee and donuts with our extended families. I do believe those weekly visits kept us all centered and continually moored to the idea of being good.

The world back in the '60s and '70s was so much better, in so many ways. I do not think it was a coincidence that our lives were better when our families were gathering regularly in faith and fellowship.

I miss our church and the families we shared it with, and I will love them both forever. The world is in trouble once again and I believe only God can save us now.

The Greatest Decade Ever
For the Families of 1955 -1965

If you were raised in the 1950s or 1960s, I'm pretty sure you already know how lucky you were. What you may not know is if you were a member of a family between 1955 and 1965, you actually lived in the greatest era of the family ever. That was a very short window of time where something happened that had never happened before, and will never happen again. It was the golden era of the family.

You see, it was the only period in history that the families did everything together. This was a result of a set of unusual circumstances that all convened at the same time. Music, television and movies of that time were all designed to appeal to all members of the family. More important, there was only one, singular method of delivery of this content in almost every American household.

Most American families possessed only 1 radio, 1 television, and had access to only 1 movie screen (at the local movie theatre). Consider this: for that brief one period of history, our entire family enjoyed, the same songs, TV shows and movies together.

MUSIC: World War 2 (and the Korean War) had ended. It was a time for a new beginning. The era of the "Big Bands" and crooners was coming to a close. In

1954, "Rock Around the Clock" burst onto the music scene ushering in the new sound. A pleasant mixture of Pop and Rock and Roll was designed for our parents and us "baby boomers." We had just one radio over the kitchen sink and out of that magic little box came a strange mixture of Elvis, Buddy Holly, Frank Sinatra, and Jerry Lee Lewis.

At the same time, the classic songs like "Mack the Knife," "Mr. Sandman" and Yellow Rose of Texas would randomly pop up on the playlist. The whole family enjoyed a keen balance between the two styles. Parents and kids alike, at least, appreciated the other's favorites. My mom and I both loved Elvis. This peaceful co-existence was perhaps out of necessity as, again, there was only one radio in the house. There were no private sources of music. No one had a (personal) transistor radio yet and, even more important, there were no headsets (singular ear phones) that allowed you to block out other family members.

Television: Although TV programing started in the late 40's and early 50's family shows like Dragnet, Lassie, Superman, Twilight Zone, Perry Mason and Gunsmoke were family staples almost immediately. These family shows (not called sitcoms yet) continued to flourished in the 1960's with newer shows like Andy Griffith, Beverly Hillbillies and I Dream of Jeannie arriving at a steady pace. Popcorn was popped, Kool-Aid was made as families gathered on and around the living room couch for some quality family time. We laughed so much together. Again, there was just one television, there were no TVs in the kids' bedrooms and, thank God, there were no cell phones.

Movies: Oh, what a treat it was when our mom and dad took us to the Schine Theatre on West 2nd Street in Oswego, NY. We couldn't afford to go every week, as it cost between 5 and 10 dollars to bring the entire family out to see the big screen. (This included food.) It was breathtaking as that giant screen and that booming sound transported all of us to different times and places together. There was only one screen and it was usually showing a Disney classic. The place was full of families.

Sure, it was huge to us but even more so for our parents who were raised with just the excitement you could derive from listening to a radio show. I especially remember those cold and snowy Saturdays where we would enter the movies in the daylight and come back out onto the streets in the dark with the bright marquee lights flashing. It was magical.

The enchanting brief era of the family all came to a rather sudden end in the mid 1960s when the Beatles and the British Invasion. Music had become the primary vehicle used, for a young and restless generation to protest. Of course, there were also those questionable lyrics of "Sex, drugs and rock and roll" that our parents wished to have no part of.

At this same time, personal (transistor) radios and ear phones were invented and used. Many households got multiple TVs and movie theatres proceeded to add multiple showings and screens. Content produced got so "questionable" that a new rating system would be needed that would inevitably come to separate the families.

Yes, it was a sad series of events that led to the demise of our families as we knew them, during that wonderful decade spanning the '50s and '60s. But, consider this: how lucky were we to have experienced that precious period of time at all?

Think about this, out of approximately 12,000 generations, we were blessed enough to be raised by the greatest generation of all time. I would say that fact alone makes us the luckiest generation.

Our kids or grandkids will never be able to comprehend the concept of one source of music, TV shows and movies everyone enjoyed by everyone at the same time. Yes, we were the lucky ones as our families came together for that one decade to sing, laugh and love.

Of course, it would be foolish for me not to mention the most important factors of all were that we all sat down and ate our meals together and we always went to church, together, on Sundays.

I do think it's important for us to pass down these stories to our kids and grandkids in hopes that there will be a tiny chance they may see the value and beauty of that precious time. Perhaps, they will try their best to rekindle it, even if in only the slightest ways. Thank God we actually got to live that dream in our lifetimes.

The Tape Recorder

In 1958, in the heart of downtown Oswego, there was a store named Rudolph's Jewelers. At that intersection of West 1st and Bridge, lay the cornerstone for "The House of Music" of the Trionfero family on 5th Street Road. A family decision was to be made at the end of the 1950s that would come to affect all of our musical lives, especially mine.

Our mom wanted a new television and our dad, who loved music, wanted this new contraption called a reel-to-reel tape recorder. It was so new it was only available at that jewelry store. Television was just coming into its own at this time and our mom wanted to be part of that gold rush. Our father had a different view of television at its inception. He called it, "The one-eyed monster." He, prophetically proclaimed, "It would be the demise of the family." How right he was about that very first screen that would invade our homes and families and start to disconnect us all.

After a long "discussion," Dad won that battle and music entered our lives with a bang. We listened to music all day every day. Although he didn't play an instrument, he had a passion for songs and singing. I can still picture him on Sunday mornings singing his favorite Hank Williams song, "Kaw-Liga."

It made him so happy. Music was almost like an addiction to him. He would often come home from work with boxes of records that he borrowed from his co-workers to record over the weekend. I remember many a long night with him trying to capture as many songs as he could into that magical box before he had to return that vinyl gold the next morning.

All of us grew up loving music, especially my brother Marshall and myself. I remember, as a little kid, banging my head on our couch and singing along to the songs pretending I was the star on stage. To this day, Marshall and I frequently swap songs via email.

My dad would bring our tape recorder to our relatives' houses for parties and sing alongs. There was so much laughter. He would play a game with us kids, allowing us to record ourselves talking, as long as we didn't repeat ourselves. It would be the 1st time I would hold a microphone in my hand.

That tape recorder planted the seed in me to love music. I pounded on my mom's pots and pans for drums until she, reluctantly, got me a toy drum set. Marshall would eventually buy me my first real drum. My Aunt Di would sing Elvis and my Aunt Bev gave me my 1st guitar to play along.

Music was the air that I breathed in that house of music. It wasn't too long before that music spilled over into our adjacent garage, when my first band began to practice. Perhaps, it was one of the very 1st garage bands in Oswego, NY.

Music has been my entire life and my career. It's all because of that house of music on 5th Street Road. To this day, on that very same garage, hangs a Side by Side sign from my first band. My dad put it up there.

My proudest accomplishment of my career was how proud my dad was of me. I also want to thank my brother-in-law, Fred Maxon, for keeping that sign on his garage, even after a recent remodeling. It is appreciated, Fred.

I sometimes think back to that fateful decision made in 1958 and I thank God that my dad brought that tape recorder home from his trip to the Jewelry store. Thank you, Dad.

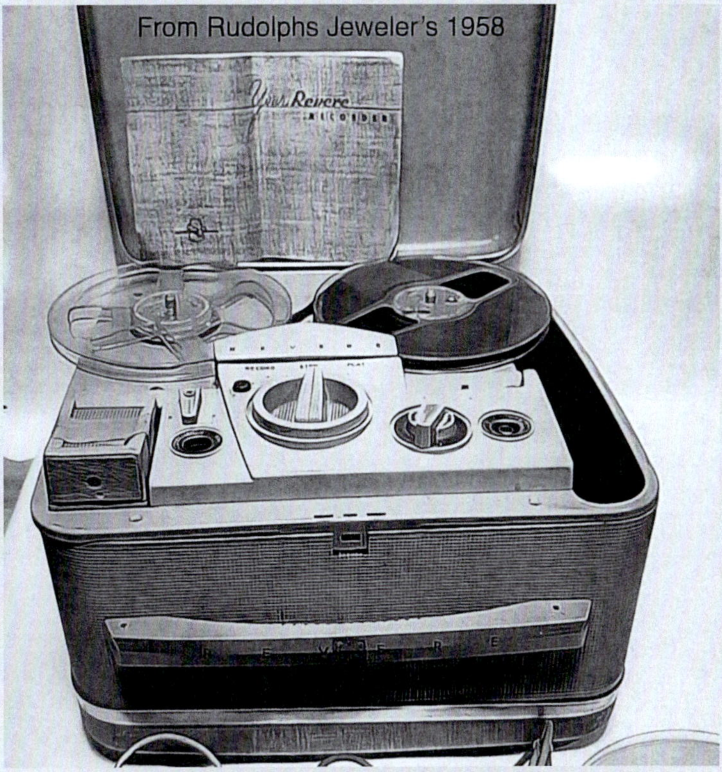

From Rudolphs Jeweler's 1958

Side by Side

Picnic in the Parking Lot

The most important question about our family's Fourth of July picnic was never about fireworks or who's bringing the potato salad. The only thing that truly mattered was if our Uncle Charles was going to be there. You can call it a picnic or you can call it a reunion, but to the Trionfero, Avery and Mills families, it was always about our family patriarch, Charles Avery. July fourth was his birthday. Even though he was only my uncle, he would be the only grandfather I ever knew.

My fondest memories as a kid growing up in the 1960s were those July 4th picnics. My Gram, Agnes Gorton, and my Uncle Charles and Aunt Grace were the nucleus of our family. It may not seem so now but, back in those days, the family was pretty spread-out all-over Oswego County. Scriba, Oswego and Phoenix might has well have been hundred miles apart. So, it was always very special to get together for fun, family and food. The epicenter of these amazing memories was the Avery's brick house on Jacksonville Road, now called County Route 55.

The picnics started back in the 1950s at Bayshore Grove, but over the years they migrated to Fair Haven, Nestle Park and, my favorite, the Avery homestead on County Line Road in Phoenix. There was food galore. Everyone brought their favorite dishes. My mom and all of our aunts always worried there would not be enough food, but, somehow, there was always enough "loaves and fishes" to feed the 5000.

The games were fun. It was quite remarkable to see our parents and elders of the family let their hair down and toss an egg or get soaked by a water balloon. There was always a family wiffle ball game and my dad and uncles would, inevitably, end up pitching horseshoes. We all knew there would eventually be a "high stakes" poker game for nickels, dimes and glasses of beer. I was so proud when I became old enough to earn my "rite of passage" to sit at that picnic table with the adults.

In the 1980s our family picnics got even more fun as JTS Music (our family business) would provide the music to liven things up a bit. There was always a lot of singing. It was around this same time when my wife and my own five kids were introduced to this sacred family tradition. I'd like to think it was as magical to them as it was to me. I know it was to my younger cousin, Shawna, as we still reminisce about it to this day.

There were so many factors that made these family picnics special, but at their core, the one common denominator was my Uncle Charles. He was different from my dad and my other Italian uncles. He was adventurous and spontaneous. He always had a positive outlook. Anytime you asked him how he was, he would respond, "Well, I saw the sun come up." I recall one picnic when the day got very hot, he hadn't brought his swim suit so he asked for scissors and proceeded to cut off his pants.

My fondest memory of all that I will NEVER forget was "The picnic in the parking lot." Somewhere back in the mid- 1960s, we arrived at Fair Haven State Park late in the morning, on a very hot day, for our annual celebration. That's when it happened! We found out quickly that our favorite location on the bluffs (and every other spot) was occupied. As we all sat in the parking lot with our caravan of crowded cars, my parents and the others were panicked and bickering about whose fault it was for this predicament. What were we going to do?

During this actual "heated discussion," I witnessed the most incredible sight. My Uncle Charles began to quietly unload his packed car. He placed his picnic basket, ice chest and bags onto the nearby patch of grass in the center of the parking lot. Then, like a general in the middle of battle, he began to shout orders. "Grab that picnic table, move this car and borrow that grill." The next thing we knew, our entire family was set up on that tiny grass island in the middle of this giant parking lot.

We had a blast. We never stopped giggling the whole day. In fact, we were closer to the beach, bathrooms and a nearby field we could play ball in. There's an old saying about when life throws you lemons you make lemonade. Well, our Uncle Charles was the master. We were all so happy and proud. It was my most spectacular July 4th ever.

I'm not sure if it was the passing of my Uncle Charles, in 1987, or the slow evaporation of the family, but these picnics are no more. Sure, it's sad, but I do have these wonderful memories of our family's special picnics. More important I am sure that, in some way, our Uncle Charles' influence lingers in me and in the rest of his family in one way or another.

He taught his family the most valuable lesson of all. When it came to our family picnics, it was never about the fireworks, food or even the location. It was always and only about the family being together. His legacy lives on and he will never be forgotten as he was our family's fireworks. Afterall, Charles F. Avery was born on the 4th of July.

31

Charles F Avery

Shawna Avery & Joe Trionfero

The Yellow Kitchen Table

My earliest memories of my childhood are playing under the yellow kitchen table at my grandmother Agnes Gorton's house in Scriba, NY. This would be during the mid 1950s. My grandparents, parents, aunts and uncles would all sit around that table drinking coffee, smoking cigarettes, "kibitzing" (talking) and laughing with each other. Every weekend and holiday we would gather, without calling ahead, around that kitchen table to be "family."

I remember, as a very young child, sitting under that table, with Rex the dog, scribbling on the bottom of it. (It was allowed.) I actually can recall falling asleep between everyone's feet in the smoke-filled kitchen listening to the coffee cups clanging on the table top and the muttering of several voices.

That table is priceless to me and has been in my family for over 70 years now. It was purchased in the mid 1950s at Goldbergs furniture and appliance store on W.1st Street in Oswego, NY. It only spent about 10 years in Scriba when my Grampa Phil died and my Gram moved in with us on 5th Street Road.

The table then moved to her sister's home on County Line Rd in Phoenix, NY, where it spent the next 25 years at my Aunt Grace and Uncle Charles' house. They were more like grandparents to me and I loved that those weekly family gatherings, around that table, continued throughout my childhood.

After the passing of Uncle Charles, Aunt Grace gave me the table (knowing my attachment to it). I promptly took that yellow table back to Oswego to my dad's home, as it seemed only fitting that the patriarch of our family should have it. That's where that table stayed for the next 35 years, until we lost our dad to Covid, in January of 2021.

Our Dad had continued our weekly family get togethers, but he did move them to Tuesday nights accommodating everyone's increasingly busy lives. My sister Rosanne and her husband Fred carry on the weekly gatherings to this day.

If only that table could talk. It would tell of the millions of moments it has seen over the generations. So much more than meals, coffee and cigarettes were shared over that table top. Families were visiting, confiding, consoling, laughing and crying with each other on a weekly basis around that table.

As for that yellow table, it now sits at my house, just on the other side of this computer that I am writing this on. It resides in my (heated) garage, my happy place. To this day, even though we have a pretty nice house, when our big family comes over to Gramma and Grampa's, they, often, never even make it into the house. Our family still tends to gather around that yellow table.

I don't know all the answers for the troubles in the world, but I guarantee the starting point, to making the world better, would be for all of us to start gathering around our kitchen tables again.

Same Table 70 years later
(that's me, my mom is holding)

I Love My Cousins

If you were lucky enough to grow up in the '50s and '60s in Oswego, NY, you know just how important your cousins were to you (especially if you were Italian). Our Trionfero story began at 36 Herrick Street, where Marcello and Angelina Trionfero raised their family. Rose, Frances and Joseph were their three kids who created this amazing connection between one big family. Those three Trionfero kids married and a lasting bond was created between those twelve Italian cousins.

The Families of Carmen & Rose Ruggio   Tony & Fran DiGaetano and Joseph and Inez Trionfero were connected forever.

The Cousins:
Frank, Vicky, Angie, Donna, and Christine (Ruggio)
Kathy, Anthony and Mark (DiGatano)
Marshall, Joseph, Ken and Rosanne (Trionfero)

We grew up close. We played, we sang and we did sports. We had picnics, trips and dinners together (so many dinners). We celebrated baptisms and weddings and we mourned at wakes and funerals, together. We were one, the line separating our three families was always invisible. To us twelve, "cousin" was a term we used for our extra special siblings.

There are a few reasons our family was, perhaps, a bit closer than most, as we are an extended family of intense love! Our Grandparents (Marcello and Angelina) died within three days of each other, bonding their three kids even closer than most others. Our gram passed first and then our grampa died of a broken heart a few days later. Then our oldest cousin, Frank, passed away at a very young age, which drew the next generation closer as well. No matter what, it was the laughter and joy that our families retained, despite these losses, that I remember most.

Our moms laughed and giggled as they visited and cooked to express their love for their families. Our fathers worked hard (so hard) at their jobs to provide a better life for all of their children. We all helped each other and we all prayed for each other. We went to church together and supported each others' families in every way we could.

We cousins played games, rode bikes and, best of all, had sleepovers, where we stayed up much too late without our parents knowing. (They knew.) We were saddened at dusk when the streetlights came on, as it signified the end of the day and the conclusion of our fun. But not to worry, as I remember playing catch on the street with my cousin Anthony at first light the next morning.

I remember thinking we were kings of the world. There were Little League games, trips to watch the Syracuse Chiefs and, once we even made the pilgrimage to New York City to see the Yankees play. We actually saw "The Mick" hit a home run.

My cousins Anthony and Kathy introduced us to The Beatles, which inspired me to want to be in a band. We cousins remain close. To this day, I never spell my last name out without saying F as in "Frank" always, in honoring my oldest cousin.

My fondest memory will always be the family on the patio under the grapevine behind 36 Herrick. It was Heaven to have our parents sitting in that circle visiting, laughing and drinking wine as we kids played in the yard or climbed that cherry tree. My dad even referred to Heaven as "Under the grapevine," where we would all be together again."

We are all aging pretty fast now and we are getting up there in age. Yes, it's sad to see us all starting to get older and sick. Although those darn streetlights are beginning to come on, we cousins have no fear since Frank, Donna and Linda will show us the way. They are saving our spots under the grapevine.

My Big Brother

As I started to write my stories, I was reminded of what a profound influence my big brother Marshall (Trionfero) had on my life. Although I see him most every Tuesday night at our family dinners, at our sister's house, I never tell him. I don't know if it's a "guy thing" or an "Italian thing."

In the 1960s, if you grew up in the country, you did not have many friends. Our dad worked at the Papermill many hours. Until our younger brother and sister were born, Marshall and I were best friends and inseparable.

Every step of the way, all the things I'm good at or love, he is the one that instilled them into me. As most of Oswego knows, music has been a gigantic part of my life. "Brother Marshall" taught me to how to listen to, understand and appreciate music by first educating me with those albums of the '60s.

In sports, he taught me to catch a ball, make a basket and throw a spiral. He led the way for me in every school, he was so smart. I cannot tell you how many times my teacher asked me if I was going to be a smart is my older brother. Yeah, sometimes it would sting a bit, but it didn't matter, because I knew he was always looking out for me.

He got me my first job at Vona Shoes and showed me the ropes. He was best man at my wedding. I followed his path of good citizenship, joining the Oswego Jaycees. He made me a Syracuse Chief's fan and talked me into buying season tickets. (He rarely misses a game.) Probably the most important thing he taught me was to be a good person.

I will never forget the 1st real, hard lesson he imposed on me. We were both working at the shoe store and I had just got my license to drive. When backing out of a parking spot behind the store, I sideswiped a car that belong to May Tompkins. (She was the owner of Barry's Outlet in the '70s.) I left the scene and went back into the store to see if my brother could cover me.

He immediately made me go over to her store and confess, apologize and offer to pay for the damage. I will never forget, as long as I live, that Ms. Tompkins told me not to worry about it, she just appreciated me coming to her and telling her the truth.

I truly cannot say how much I appreciate my mentor. Marshall is now, and always will be my big brother and my best friend.

Trionfero Family and the Blizzard of 66

Back in the 1950s there was a great (scary) movie called *"The Day the Earth Stood Still."* It was a sci-fi drama about aliens landing in Washington, D.C. to promote world peace. The catch was they shut down the entire planet in doing so. Everything came to a stop.

I think about that movie sometimes and I reflect on the two times in my life that the world did actually shut down. The most recent time was, of course, during Covid. The planet stood still as unimaginable losses happened while we all had to stay home and watch it play out in real time, feeling helpless. The only other time that the Trionfero's world was shut down was during the Blizzard of 1966. That time it was so different.

During that storm there was a peaceful feeling of content and safety within our home that I will never forget. It was like the great feeling a kid gets from a "snow day," times ten. The world was shut down, factories, schools and roads were CLOSED. Mother Nature saw to it and our family enjoyed it immensely within our loving refuge. Here are the reasons why that blizzard has such fond memories:

My dad had a snow day and that never happened. It was so weird to see him wandering around the house doing nothing. There were extra cups of coffee and

43

Mom and Dad chatted at the kitchen table. It was so surreal and wonderful.

Mom baked cookies and smiled a lot. She got us kids dressed to go out and play knowing, full well, we would be back in within minutes. When we Trionfero brothers eventually got outside we were so proud that we could touch the roof of our house while standing on the snow bank.

My fondest memory of that historic storm was the goodness that I witnessed from humanity, neighbors helping neighbors. The thing that stands out in my mind the most was the Falise family rising to the occasion. They were one of the first families to have "Ski Doos" (snowmobiles) and they came to the rescue. They helped everyone, running up and down 5th Street Road, delivering bread and milk and medicine to their neighbors.

Of course, there were many other families that helped their neighbors that day, but those Falise boys were special because they were our friends. Since Michael, Stanley and Stephen were the same ages as me and my brothers Marshall and Ken, it made it all the more special.

I never really connected the dots, but it dawned on me what a gift that their family had given ours. The reason that the terrible storm holds such great

44

memories for my family was because their family allowed us to feel safe and secure. They took that "Love Thy Neighbor" thing seriously. Yes, the earth stood still that day but the human heart and the spirit of love continued in perpetual motion.

It was a special time for sure. How wonderful it would be to have it that way again, today. Neighbors looking out for each other, in a time of need, regardless of their race, religion or party affiliation. I am pretty sure God would approve.

45

Tuesdays With Gram

For the better part of the 1980s, I spent every Tuesday afternoon at St Luke's Apartments on West 1st Street in Oswego visiting my grandmother Agnes Mills Gorton. A full decade before, "Tuesdays with Morrie" (the Mitch Albom book) came out, I would drive from Baldwinsville to Oswego once a week to have an egg and olive sandwich, a bowl of homemade popcorn and a bottle of Coca-Cola.

More important, I would enjoy a few hours of great conversation with my best friend, my Gram. She wasn't your normal grandmother by any measure. First and foremost, she helped raised us four Trionfero kids. Because Gram practically lived with us, she helped care for us, taught us and loved us. Most of my earliest memories include her.

My mom and my Gram were also best friends. I can still picture the two of them sitting at our kitchen table drinking coffee and smoking Old Gold cigarettes. They'd be talking about family and friends, the day's news and, of course, the obituaries.

During the '80s my business (JTS Music) needed me to work weekends but allowed me to take those precious Tuesdays for myself. These lunches

46

afforded me the opportunity to unwind from the pressures of my job and escape to my hideaway in apartment 214.

Of course, being a young man, I had many options for my free time, but I found myself lured to that quiet and peaceful refuge with the Coke in the fridge and my spot on the couch saved. You see, my Gram was special. She stayed up on current events and loved to talk, teach and listen. Sure, from time to time, we'd gossip about family and complain about the world, but what I remember most was confiding in this special lady, my problems and even some of my deepest secrets.

She listened and more importantly, she never judged me, not once. I was Catholic and, to be honest, talking to her was better than going to confession at my church. Her love and support for me was unlimited and unconditional. I found such a sense of calmness in that quiet and safe space.

My Gram was funny, a real spit-fire who never minced words. She took pleasure in telling it like it was. Some of her favorite sayings that displayed this honesty were, "He doesn't know if he's on horseback or afoot," "The only thing new at that wedding was the cake," "Why would I go to their funeral, they're not going to mine," and my favorite, "He'd complain if he got hung with a new rope."

We would often take rides around Oswego County to revisit her old homes and haunts, along with any other places that held fond memories from her past. I'll never forget the time I took her to visit my Aunt Beulah (Czerow) on Rathburn Road. When my aunt came out onto her front steps, squinted and asked, with a shocked voice, "Aggie is that you," to which my Gram responded with a casual, "Well, I ain't dead yet." My aunt did give my Gram a parting gift that day, a tiny white cross that she had crocheted. As soon as the car door shut, Gram placed it on the dash and said, "You keep this, what in heavens name am I going to do with it." Forty years later, that cross still sits on my dash.

One of my fondest memories was on my 40th birthday. When I arrived to her place, she already had her purse in her hand and her apartment key wrapped around her wrist, ready to go. We were only headed one block west, to Dufore's jewelry store, where she had planned to buy me a special gift. When we arrived, we were greeted by the proprietor, Mr. Dufore (the original), who, upon my Gram's request, began showing us the St. Joseph's medals displayed in one of his many shiny glass cases. It was much more than she could afford, on her very fixed income, but she was hell-bent on buying it. After picking one out she "suggested" that Mr. Dufore engrave the medal for her grandson.

When offered the unlimited options of what he could fit on the back of that medal, I said to the jeweler to simply engrave the word "Gram" with her birthday, 5/13/11. My Gram responded with a very touching, "You damn fool." It was one of those precious moments.

When we returned to her apartment, as I thanked her for the third time for the very special gift, I finally thought to question, "Why a St Joseph's medal," she was never a very religious person. She responded immediately with something I will never forget. "The world's going to hell in a handbasket and this will help protect you." At the time I thought that perhaps the "old woman" was a tad crazy, as the world seemed pretty good to me. Still, I was happy and proud to put that medal on… every day.

Fast forward, and I do mean FAST forward, 40 years later, and now, when I put this medal on, I'm the Grampa and it turns out my Gram was right. The world certainly appears to be going to hell in a hand basket.

These days I reflect a lot about those Tuesday lessons she gave me, as I was being educated in life without even knowing it. She taught me so much, but on that particular day, back in the 1980s, she taught me the most valuable lesson of all. One I would still remember decades later. She taught me to always remember, "It's better to have faith in God than trust in man." To this day I still try to pass on some of my Gram's wisdom to her great-great-grandchildren.

By the way, at 72, I am the very same age that "old woman" was when I was making my weekly pilgrimages to Oswego. Turns out, she wasn't that old after all, but she sure was wise.

I remember my Gram's advice and think, how funny that my strong faith comes from a woman who really wasn't that religious. The fact remains I trusted her then and I trust her now, as she was my best friend. I think of her often and I do smile every morning as I drink my Coke and remember those Tuesday afternoons with Gram.

50

Grampa Days

"Tickle Town" was the forbidden phrase that our grandkids were warned never to say unless, of course, they wished to go there and be tickled mercilessly. It was a place they would frequently end up whenever they visited Gramma and Grampa's. Despite the clear warnings and impending consequences, every one of our 11 grandkids dared to test the waters and say the forbidden phrase. When they did say it, they would be tickled until they could simply say the magic words, "I don't want to go to Tickle Town." The laughter was just as magical.

Tickle Town was one of the many games and activities we created and played together during those 25 glorious years of "Grampa Days" at the Trionfero homestead on Gettman Drive. There was also "take a step back," "coloring contest," "giant water slide," (with a tarp and garden hose) "talent contest," "crate ball," "what doesn't fit," and of course the annual highlight of the "Grampa Day Graduations."

Although she doesn't know it, "Grampa Days" were actually inspired by our 1st grand kid Gabriella. It was early one morning, in 1998, when Denise and I were sleeping and the 4-year-old was in the bedroom next door for her very first sleepover. I had no plan or intention of starting a 25-year tradition of Tuesdays with Grampa, but on that fateful morning this kid made her way into the center of our bed around 5 AM. She wasn't scared, she just wanted to play and get the adventures started at Gramma and Grampa's.

Although I relented and let her cuddle in the bed between us, I pleaded with the child to let us sleep just a little longer. When the "quiet game" didn't work, I simply tried to tell her to go back to sleep every time she would ask me, yet, another question. After many of these, she hit me with a question that I did not see coming and would change the course of history for our Trionfero clan. The monumental question? The four-year-old innocently asked, "Grampa, you know why I love you?" As tired as I was, she immediately had my attention. I said, "No, why?" She said, "Because you play with me." My feet hit the floor in less than five seconds and the games commenced at Gettman Drive on that very first Grampa Day.

The instant I fully realized the significance that I played in these kids' lives, I decided to devote the remainder of my life to being the best, most fun, Grampa of all time. Grampa Days were created. Every Tuesday during summers and breaks, and every Friday night during the school year, our tribe would gather at Gramma and Grampa's for laughter, love and pizza. We would always have meals together and go around the table taking turns sharing the highlights of our past week. Our Friday gatherings were called Gramma Nights. (She did all the work)

I'd be lying if I didn't admit to a hidden factor in the back of my mind and in a secret compartment in the center of my heart. I wasn't the best dad that I should have or could have been. I suppose, like many parents, I was too busy working and raising my kids to really enjoy them. Being a self-employed entertainer, I worked every weekend of my kids' short journey through childhood. It's one of my few regrets. I vowed I would do better this time around for our 11 grandkids.

Grampa Days only had three rules: No Fighting, No Phones and No TV. We always made our own fun. The special Tuesdays always started with lunch at noon and ended at five when the parents of our three local families would show up to collect their little ones. We had one family living in the Saratoga area and therefore we only had those two kids on special occasions, but when we did it was extra special.

Grampa Days were planned completely by the kids, including the hourly snack breaks that the parents "appreciated" so much. There were weekly cookouts, kickball games and hide and seek adventures. It was so much fun, often the neighborhood kids would ask to join. (It was probably the hourly snacks.) Over the years, we invented our own games, many challenging our grandkids to use their creativity without accessing technology. We told stories, made movies and even wrote our own "Birthday Song."

Of course, we had outings, field trips and special events. We had so many picnics. Our annual mecca to Rochester to Sea Breeze would be the crown jewel of the summer of fun. It was common for me to have at least a half of dozen little kids each week, including changing a few diapers. When our brood got to over six kids, we were forced to stay and play at Gettman as we had too many kids to fit in one car. One Sea Breeze trip, to Rochester, I actually rode the entire trip cramped into the storage compartment, behind the third seat, with the picnic basket and ice chest, so we didn't have to take two cars.

Although, over the years, we had hundreds of outings at some of the premier (and very expensive) fun spots in CNY, the greatest Grampa Day of all time would be the "Mud Day" of 2006. It happened right at the end of my street. It cost us no money, but that day was unanimously voted "number one" by those six kids who experienced that day in the mud. It was a mild Veterans Day; schools were closed and the gates to "Tickle Town" were wide open. There was a nearby housing development being built that included a retainer pond as a catch basin for the area. The required fence had not been put up yet, thus we had access to this amazing pond and its "mud beach."

They played all day. We scurried home shortly before 5pm to get cleaned up before the parents could see the mess we had created. They were so dirty, that in order to keep my marriage intact, I decided to hose them all off in the front yard to get the first four layers of dirt off outside. Needless to say, one of the moms came early and was quite surprised at the scene of my makeshift shower in our front yard. Looking back, I do wonder what the neighbors thought?

The little ones have all grown now. It's so hard to believe their ages range between 14 and 30. Where did my time go? So many memories were made. I hope our 11 angels will remember them fondly. My greatest wish is that these special memories will remain and create a lifetime bond between the cousins that will last forever. Not an easy task in an era where the family, as we know it, is dispersing. It turns out, my initial intention of offering these special days as a gift of a lifetime to my grandchildren turned out to be a gift of a lifetime to me. The one thing I truly hope they realize the most is, I was never (ever) a babysitter. I was only their playmate and teacher looking to share another game or adventure. I cherished every second we shared.

I must thank the three people in my life (and in my heart) who were the inspiration behind this tradition of love and fun. My dad, the actual inventor of Tickle Town. (In the 1950s it was called "Cheech a doo.") My first cousin Anthony DiGaetano who made me realize how close 1st cousins could (and should) be. Lastly, I must thank my wife Denise who, while I was building and running our family business, raised our five kids, pretty much on her own. I only did it one day a week with our grand kids and I was exhausted. Denise did it for our five kids, 24/7 for thirty years, and never missed a beat. We all know who the real hero is. (Denise worked all the while at Syracuse University, a career to which she invested an amazing 34 years. While there, she nurtured a few extra kids of her own, making a difference in so many of her students' lives.)

I'm not sure what Heaven will look like when I get there but I'm thinking it might look a lot like "Tickle Town."

"Love Lives in a Smile"
Grampa Joe Trionfero

56

For: Anna, Theo, Matteo, Meagan, Joseph, Shane, Olivia, Ben, Mattison, Becca and Gabriella.

"Mud Day" November 2006

Grampa Days

Gabriella makes 1st trip to "Tickle Town"

57

"Love Lives in a Smile"
(Love is the Answer)

Dad's number one saying was our family motto, "Love Lives in a Smile." Our father was a simple and soft-spoken man that everyone loved and respected. He took time to stop and smell the roses and would always pause to help others. He was aware of the beauty and love that surrounded him. He taught his kids to be kind and thankful. Dad valued those things that made us smile or laugh out loud. These are stories of love that made me smile and yes, sometimes, even burst into laughter.

The Dog That Served in WWII

During my years of performing shows at hundreds of senior homes around the state, I have had the pleasure of meeting the most interesting people with some of the most amazing and heartwarming stories. One such encounter was when my grandkids and I met Marjorie Williams at the Waterville RCC in Waterville, New York. (Formerly the Harding Nursing Home.)

Mrs. Williams, a 97-year-old resident, approached the stage at the end of the show, with the aid of her walker, to tell us how much she enjoyed it. I noticed she was having a difficult time navigating with her walker as she was also, gingerly, holding onto a picture of a dog in her right hand. You could see the picture held great value as she had it wrapped within a separate sheet of paper. She thought my grandkids, who were also part of the show, would enjoy a "nice story" about a dog.

She proceeded to tell us the story of Shackles, the dog who served with her brother on his warship during WWII at Pearl Harbor. What she introduced as a "cute little story" about a dog had me riveted within seconds. She began to tell Shackles' saga.

Marge told of how one of the sailors had snuck the dog aboard the ship after a "night out on the town" during one of its brief periods of "being in a port for shore leave." She spoke of how the dog was found the next day in a lifeboat on the ship, under a tarp, covered in tar. Finally, Mrs. Wells softly spoke of how the ship's captain was going to have the stray, "put down" until the ship's doctor saved it when he said, "There was nothing wrong with that dog that a little cleaning up wouldn't fix."

Shackles became the ship's loyal mascot and served alongside those brave sailors of the U.S. Navy for the duration of the war. Shackles was, in fact, wounded at war once, "when a big oaf of a sailor stepped on him and broke his leg."

As she was telling her story, with a quivering voice, anyone could see that this dog, and his tale, meant the world to her. She teared up, especially near the end of the story when describing how, after the war, he returned to her home on Osborne Street. "That dog spent his remaining 14 years in Waterville, New York."

Marjorie lamented on the sailors who, after the war, traveled from all over the country to her little town to, "visit their former shipmate, Shackles."

Realizing the priceless value of the story we just heard, I asked her to repeat it so I could record it on my phone. With a huge smile, she proudly pulled out a typed copy of the story that she treasured as much as her pictures.

Needless to say, I remembered that story and so did my grandkids who, by the way, never looked at their phones once as she was telling it.

The Perfect Game (Almost)

Back in the mid-1960s, at the Babe Ruth Stadium at the Fort Ontario baseball fields, a rookie pitching star named Gigsy Enwright was pitching the game of his life. He took to the mound for his Lions Club team late that afternoon for the seven-inning game.

Gigsy James Enwright had retired 20 batters in a row, only to face one final batter for his perfect game. His opponent was a measly little rookie, Joe Trionfero, the second baseman for the Masons. Like the rest of my team, I was scared to death, as he was bringing the heat throughout the entire game. He was clearly in the zone and he happened to be the only southpaw we had ever faced. One other thing; he was smiling!

Anyone who knows Gigsy Enwright knows he was always smiling that coy little smile that exposes the warmth in that big heart of his. On that day, from the batter's box, he looked more like the cat standing in front of the canary, just before breakfast. I would be lying if I told you I knew the pitch-by-pitch of that at-bat, but what I do remember is I got a hit. It was a little Texas leaguer just over the second baseman's head. I broke up a perfect game. I did it. It was to be the highlight of my short sports career. For once, I was the hero.

63

At first, I didn't even think about that Enwright boy's feelings. He had already achieved so many milestones at a young age. He was a natural born athlete and everyone knew it and respected him for it. He had so many great games. You see, Gigsy came from sports royalty. His older brothers, Leo and Fran, had already established reputations for being of a certain sports pedigree. What would it matter to him if, just this one time, he missed making another milestone. But truth be told, it did matter. I felt a little bad inside. There were three reasons.

1. Gigsy was a good kid. Although he was one of those dreaded St. Johns' kids, as we got older, we became friends. He was a kind and gentle person. He was always loyal to his family and friends. His wife Judy told me a beautiful story that "Gigs" had shared with her about the time he hit two home runs off his best friend Bodie Schaffer. As he rounded third base Bodie walked off the mound to shake Gigsy's hand. These was just the kind of kids that the fifth Street gang produced. They were all fine young men.
2. I should have never even hit that ball. I was shaking in my spikes, and I am pretty sure my eyes were closed when I hit it. He was the great athlete, I was not.
3. Last, and most important, The Enwrights were kind of like family. We were connected through the Ruggios of Herrick Street. My Uncle Carm

and Aunt Rosie were Gigsy's aunt and uncle too. Okay, we weren't like twins, but there was a connection.

The Trionferos always respected and had a fondness for the Enwrights. In Oswego in the 1960s that's just how Italian families worked. We knew his entire family and followed the lives of Leo, Cecelia, Fran, James, Dan, Theresa and Kathy. Kathy would end up marrying my cousin Richie/Archie. These were all good, decent people.

His Mom, Frances is the matriarch of the entire city of Oswego. To know her is to love her. She's even attended a few of our Trionfero family reunions. Gigsy's wife, Judy Tuso Enwright, had also become a good friend over the years, as we had met many times at the school where she taught. (Trinity Catholic/St Paul's School.) When it comes to families, it doesn't get any better than The Enwrights of West Fifth Street. They were, as my dad would say, "Top shelf." We were lucky to know them, let alone to be "kind of related."

So, I did feel bad about breaking up Gigsy's perfect game. Although, over the years, at any opportunity I had, I would always tease him a little about his "almost perfect game." The truth is, although, I felt a tad of regret about ruining his special moment, it was special to me. It connected us, in a way, for a lifetime.

65

There was one more thing I remembered about that summer evening at the ballpark. No, Gigsy did not come over to shake my hand after my base hit, but he was still smiling, even after I ruined his night. That was true class and that was real respect.

The bottom line, Gigsy Enwright is truly a Good Man from a Great Family. The Perfect, however, wouldn't be his baseball game that day, but it will be the legacy that the Enwright Family will leave behind. They will forever be known as that great little family from the west side of Oswego. I am proud to have been "kind of related." They are good people.

The Only Woman to Ever Make Me Blush

During the past couple of decades, I have been doing my shows for seniors all over New York State. This includes skilled nursing, assisted living and memory care facilities. Many of these places are still home to the greatest generation.

I have entertained, laughed and learned so much from so many amazing residents. One such woman was Mary Ruth, a "Ninety something," lady who was a classy, funny and beautiful. I met her at The Elizabeth Church Manor in Binghamton, New York. When we first met, we hit it off immediately.

I found her to be personable, engaging and interesting. I found myself listening to her after my show, as she told me many of her fascinating stories. I recalled a lot of her memories, but one that stood out to me was how proud she was that her brother had been a very prominent doctor in the area. At the time, I filed this tidbit away in my memory.

Well, fast forward a year and I returned to the same facility and, to my delight, Mary Ruth was still there and she remembered me as well as I remembered her. If you have ever seen me perform before you would know that I like to have fun with my audience so, during the show, I began to tease my new friend. I introduced Mary Ruth as my old high school sweetheart. I began to construct the most amazing story you could imagine. I explained why I loved her so and our romantic history.

A key part of this story that I was making up as I was spinning my yarn, was how the two of us had met. I began telling the packed room of our very embarrassing first encounter. Using parts of her own story and memories that she shared with me on my previous visit, I started my tall tale.

I said, "I met Mary Ruth in the most embarrassing way. I was actually a patient of her brother, a very famous doctor in the area, when she unexpectedly entered into the examining room and accidentally saw me in my underwear." At this time, the entire audience burst into laughter. It was amazing. I thought I was the funniest guy in the world, but something unusual started to happen and I began to feel a bit uneasy.

The audience continued to laugh and they kept laughing. At some point I got the sense that they were actually laughing at me and not at what I said. When I looked at Mary Ruth, she was smiling ear to ear. She called me to her, using her right index finger. I moved to her slowly as I started to feel very warm and a bit uncomfortable. That's when she said it, and I quote, "Hey, my brother was a gynecologist!"

68

The entire audience erupted into laughter. I turned bright red and got just what I deserved. For many years I have been the one doing the teasing and make others do the blushing. However, this time it was my turn to blush. Mary Ruth is gone now but I will never forget her.

The Music Teacher
(Lois Scriber)

There's an old Coca-Cola commercial that coined the phrase, "I'd like to teach the world to sing in perfect harmony." Well, what the world needs now is love sweet love and I know exactly the teacher who would have been perfect to lead the way today, Lois J. Scriber.

Although, Miss Scriber taught for 35 years in the Oswego, as the old saying goes, she never worked a day in her life. I don't believe anyone on the planet loved their career more, nor had more fun, than this brilliant educator. Now that I am 72, and have spent the last 50 years in the music business, I often think back on my good fortune to have had this, "Bundle of joy" as my music teacher throughout my elementary years at Kingsford Park School.

Her resume was outstanding as she graduated from the Crane School of Music in Potsdam, New York and received her Masters from Syracuse University, in 1946. This was no easy task for anyone and, sadly, it was even harder for a woman in the 1940s. When she was our teacher in the 1960s, she already had 20 years of experience under her belt. Lois was an accomplished pianist and organist, and yet she still had the youthful exuberance of a new educator. Looking back on this, I am equally impressed and grateful.

She was a true renaissance woman, since she loved to learn, read and travel as much as she enjoyed teaching, weaving and mentoring her favorite students. Lois was a woman of strong faith, dedicating over sixty years of service to her West Baptist Church as their organist and a faithful member of the flock.

During her extensive travels she would often return to her hometown of Oswego with new things she learned or had discovered. Some of the more notable examples were the Easter program she had experienced at the Radio City Music Hall, The Handbell Ringers she discovered on a trip to the Carolinas or the Hawaiian songs she would teach her students after returning from her one-year teacher exchange program in Hawaii.

I'll never forget the songs we learned from The Sound of Music and Mary Poppins, even before we had seen the movies at our local movie theater. To this day, I never hear the songs "Do-Re-Me" or "My Favorite Things" without seeing that woman's smile.

She never stopped learning and, thank God, she had a passion to share that knowledge and teach regular kids like me. She was a trailblazer, as she started a boys and girls choir at KPS called the Kiparcants and Cantrices. I was so proud to be one of the few boys in that choir.

Miss Scriber was my favorite teacher and it wasn't just because she taught my favorite subject. She made it fun, included everyone and had an innate ability to recognize those students who could benefit from a little extra love and attention.

I felt special in her class and, come to find out, much later in life, so did everyone else. Now that's a great teacher. The real beauty of all this is that she planted thousands of seeds along her 35-year journey. I discovered this as I had the pleasure of running into a fellow classmate, Sue Lass Mahigian. Sue was the music teacher at a school in the Albany area where I was performing my "Show of Love" program. I was thrilled to learn that Susan's wonderful relationship with Lois had progressed from student to mentee to a beloved lifelong friend. How wonderful it was for me to see one of Lois Scriber's students planting her own long-lasting seeds for the next generation and carrying on her mentor's legacy. I began to wonder, if Lois Scriber had that effect on Sue and myself, how many other of her thousands of students are wandering the planet with a song in their heart that this music teacher planted.

One of Lois' favorite sayings was, "We learn by doing" and us pre-teens at KPS certainly did. Sure, we learned about music, but we also learned about life as we watched this amazing lady smile, sing, play and love. We witnessed her teaching with excitement as she continued to always learn.

We lost Lois in 2006, but I can almost guarantee you that when she reached those gates of heaven she was greeted by a choir of angels. The thing is, they weren't there to greet her with a song; they were there to ask her to join. You see, they knew that Lois had already taught the world to sing in perfect harmony. They were also grateful that she created an army of "Scriber Students" to carry on her mission of love and joy. Most of all, they were aware that she was perpetually interested in learning something new. Well, they still had some things to teach her and believe me, for Lois, that was Heaven.

Thank you, Miss Scriber, for being a great teacher and wonderful role model for future successful women like Sue. You deserve to be remembered and we will never forget you!

(Thanks to Susan Lass Mahigian for her help with this story and for providing the great picture)

73

The Lunch Lady's Dog

Over my 35 years of doing thousands of assembly programs with my Show of Love, one of the most endearing things I ever witnessed was not during one of my shows, nor did it involve a human. It was a dog, an old beagle named Daisy.

It was at a neighborhood elementary school, somewhere near Center Reach, Long Island. I had arrived early that morning, about a half hour before the students would begin to swarm the building. I checked in at the office to get my name tag and was told to drive around to the side of the school to the cafeteria door, as that is where the show would take place. I did just that and was surprised to see the door was already opened for me. Turns out, it wasn't open for me.

I got my equipment in and began to close the door when a "lunch lady" shouted, over the noise of the nearby freezers, "Leave the door open for Daisy." Not thinking too much about it, I complied and began to set up on the stage in this mid-size cafeteria. As I was hooking up my PA system, I saw the most unusual thing. An old, overweight dog, a black and brown beagle, ambled in like it owned the place, turned the corner into the kitchen area and plopped down at the end of the long lunch counter. I thought; Now that's weird, but it turns out, I had just met Daisy.

It wasn't just that a dog mysteriously let itself into a school building; it was the fact that no one paid it any mind. The three lunch ladies went on about their morning task, the custodian continued to mop up the cafeteria floor but most astounding were the dozens of kids who had now arrived to eat at their morning breakfast program. They had no reaction, as they simply stepped over the dog after getting their trays of food at the end of the counter.

My curiosity finally got the best of me, I approached one of the kids' tables that had a monitor nearby and asked, "Who was the dog?" The monitor answered it was Daisy, to which one of the older kids piped in, "Lazy Daisy." They all giggled. Someone shouted, "It was the lunch ladies' dog." I thought to myself, okay, and got back to work getting ready for my show.

I was thinking how sweet. Then, I was shocked by what I witnessed next, when the bell rang to signify the beginning of the school day. As the students began to clear their messes and leave, Daisy got up and ambled out the same door she had come in. With no direction or command, she left the building in the same uneventful manner that she arrived, all at the sound of that bell.

One of the lunch ladies immediately, and very routinely, walked over and closed the door. Now I was really invested. I just had to hear this story. I nonchalantly asked that lunch lady, "Is Daisy your dog?" She said "Nope, she's Marge's dog. She passed away a few months ago." Before I could ask my next awkward question, she concluded with, "No one's ever dared to even suggest that the sacred morning routine be broken."

The principal and teachers had to know. The lunch ladies had to step over the dog and those students needed to respect the dog's autonomy. I am pretty sure that the New York State health department would not have approved of that morning ritual either. I am guessing it continued until Marge and Daisy were reunited again.

Years later, that image of Daisy lingers in my mind. Perhaps, it's because we Trionferos are a "dog family," who firmly believe that all dogs go to heaven. Maybe it's just that cafeteria and that dog were so darn special. You see, it was more than just a simple kindness that left that door open on the side of that school building.

It was, indeed, a reverence and respect to the love between a dog and her "Mom." It was an affirmation that everyone knew they would be together again. To me, it was further proof that love transcended death.

Our Dog Coco

"Hey, You Did Our Wedding"

I love Oswego. Sure, it's my hometown and, just like many others, I have deep roots with strong family ties. The thing is, I have a pretty unique connection to the city that a lot of people can't claim. You see, I feel kind of related to the hundreds of families whose weddings I was a part of during the 1980s and 1990s. This special kinship that allowed me to feel like an honorary family member, is a direct result of the multitude of receptions that I played across the Port City back then.

For a period of twenty years, I often did three receptions every weekend at the Elks Club, Wine Creek, The Captains Lounge, and so many other wedding venues. JTS Music was my business and my key objective was to be the emcee/entertainer for the event. My mission was to keep the special day running smoothly and to make sure everyone had fun. I did this well, but I always felt my primary goal was to make sure it was a celebration that the family would remember.

Last September, I was attending Porchfest in my hometown with my brother Marshall when I was pleasantly surprised. "Hey, you did our wedding," someone shouted out to me, from a pretty fair distance. I turned and saw the (still) happy couple with giant smiles on their faces. I felt proud and honored that a couple, who trusted me with their most important day of their lives, remembered me 40 years later.

This has happened to me a few times over the years, even though many of these events were over four decades ago. In the mall, at a festival or out to dinner, I have been reminded that I was once part of their family for a day. I will admit, one time, it did sting a bit when the couple told the child with them that, "This is the man that did Gramma and Grampa's wedding." (Ouch) Still, I truly loved being a part of their special day.

I took a lot of pride in fulfilling the unique family traditions that had been passed on for generations. The introduction of the bridal party, the best man's toast and the father-daughter dance were always my favorites. The truth is I even liked the dollar dance that often took too long and allowed a silly best man the chance to cut the line and dance with the groom. (Always thinking they were the first to do it.)

Call me crazy, but I do feel the receptions back then were better. They were more family focused. Perhaps less elegant, but definitely more fun. I will never forget my aunts passing out the Italian cookies after the meal, or the bride and groom "smushing" the cake into each other's face. Both time-honored traditions. The truth is, most receptions now adays don't even include the children. I think that's a mistake. Some of my best childhood memories were of our family weddings of the 60's. It's not about elegance, up lighting or photo booths; it's about family.

It's been said often, and accurately, that the only time that families get together now are for weddings and funerals. If you exclude kids from weddings, the loss is immeasurable. I always thought it was paramount that the grandparents in attendance were announced and honored.

They say a picture is worth a thousand words and a "reception full of family" offered the professional photographer the opportunity to capture the family photos for generations to come. This reminds me of one of my proudest moments. After honoring a bride's request to gather the entire reception for a group/family photo, which was no easy task, the bride shocked and delighted me when she invited me to join in the family photo and to stand next to her. I was truly touched.

I always liked to spotlight the flower girls and ring bearers, so I would often ask them a question. I would tell them that due to their very important role in the wedding they were allowed to grant one wish for the bride and groom. I would ask them what their wish would be? Their 3 choices were: A new car….

50 thousand dollars in cash, or… a BRAND-NEW BICYCLE. You know, a lot of seniors, celebrating big anniversaries this year, have an old bike in the corner of their garages.

Another classic memory of mine; one time, I actually saved a bride from a probable injury as I literally caught her as she fell from the shoulders of some "crazy" groomsmen. A final memory, that has stayed with me since the mid '80s, came from a grandfather who, when asked, "What was the secret to a happy marriage of 60 years," responded with, "A heated porch." Everyone roared.

I also have great memories of working alongside of the room coordinators and professional photographers who were commissioned to capture those timeless memories on film. Bob Clark was one of those amazing "Picture takers." Of course, it was Mike Potter, of the Elks Club, who taught me how to run a reception. I will be forever grateful. Mike's assistant, Lucille Atkins, was one of my all-time favorite coordinators and still is one of my favorite people today. What a classy lady. My most cherished memories were the times that I got to work with my brother, Marshall, who owned JTS Video, and our dad, who was the oldest "DJ" in the city. I was also proud to work with my son Shawn, who did his own weddings, and my daughter Nicole, who ran the office.

Looking back, of course I am aware of the fact that some of those marriages didn't survive. But let us not forget that those family celebrations did take place, and many of their beautiful memories will not only survive, but last forever. And that's not nothing!

I do miss those days. But every now and then, I am pleasantly reminded of the fun I had and the important task I accomplished. Whenever some yells out, "Hey you did our wedding," I feel proud that I helped make their day, fun and memorable. Even if only for a day… "We were Family."

Marshall & Joe Trionfero

I've Been Married 537 Times

You know the old saying that a sailor has "A girl in every port"? Well, I can go one step further. I have (at least) one "wife" in several cities across New York State. (Nine just in the city of Oswego.) It all started several years ago at a nursing home I was performing at in Rochester, New York.

It was in January and, being right after the holidays, the atmosphere was sad, boring and still. I burst on to the scene in my usual fashion with microphone in hand. I noticed a vase of fresh flowers on the table in the front row and my wild imagination kicked in. I immediately played the song "Going to the Chapel" and I began to circle the table with the flowers in hand.

They say you never forget your first. My first bride, of my hundreds of one-day weddings, was Rose. We had been acquainted from previous visits and, of course, I had already told everyone that she and I dated in high school. I proceeded to played a very romantic song and I got down on one knee. I popped the question, "Rose, you're the only women I have ever loved, except Nancy, Marge and Sadie (who were seated at the table with her). Will you marry me?"

Luckily my first attempt was a success as Rose responded with a rousing "I guess so." The audience roared and I jumped up and ran to the hallway. I immediately began to play the "Bridal March" and make my grand entrance, one step at a time. Now, I know the bride was supposed to be the one to make the grand entrance, but Rose was unable to walk/move at the time, so I did it for her. It was magic! As I turned the corner, heading into that room, I saw nothing but a room full of smiles.

Everyone there, staff and residents, waited anxiously for our spontaneous wedding ceremony. I did have to play the part of the officiant and the Groom, but within minutes I pronounced us "Wife and Husband." That's when the show (contest) began. I played, and everyone had to guess, every popular Bridal song from the past 50 years. Of course, starting out with, "We've Only Just Begun" by the Carpenters. When those famous songs were depleted, I then challenged them to name every song that had a destination in it for possible honeymoon locations.

I then offered up every "traditional" reception song you could think of that we have all come to know and love. "The Polka," "The Chicken Dance," "Daddy's' Little Girl" and The Tarantella were just some of the favorites. The grand finale included many of the popular "party songs" from the 1940s to the 1980s. They sang, danced and laughed for the entire hour.

Everyone there had a day to remember, and left beaming. On that day, The Show of Love's "Wedding Themed Show" was born. I have repeated that magical day hundreds of times. Of course, I bring a wedding veil and plastic flowers to all of my special days. Sometimes, I actually bring real flowers.

It was always a spectacle. The reason for its success was it allowed a population of seniors, who had limited mobility and excitement, to use their imagination, let go and have some fun. In their minds they relived some of their favorite wedding memories. They were all invited to our wedding, reception and even the honeymoon. But, they were warned; "If there's a cowboy hat on the door handle… DON"T come in.

My favorite line of all, that I used that very first wedding, (and ever since) was, "Rose and I have an announcement to make….. Rose and I are expecting a little one….. (After the roar of laughter, I would say)… "We're getting a puppy."

I have to say my (real) wife Denise is an especially good sport about all my other weddings, especially when I arrive home with some of the most incredible perfume scents on my neck and clothes. She's okay with it all as long as I always come home to her.

So, if you're ever in the vicinity of one of my shows at a nearby senior home, stop in (no gift required). You could be "Going to the Chapel" with us. Afterall, "We've Only Just Begun."

The Perfect Couple
Barb & Bob Sugar

They are both kind, humble, caring, giving, joyful and always smiling. How in God's name did these two exceptional human beings, end up together?

Back in December of 2024, I was doing a show at The Springside at Seneca Hill when, during the show, I turned quickly and was surprised by the most wonderful sight. It was Mr. & Mrs. Bob and Barb Sugar, standing toward the back of the room smiling.

They were wearing their coats, as they had just arrived to visit someone. I think they were bringing cookies or kindness to a friend or family member. I can't explain it, but it startled me as to how it made me feel. My heart smiled as they both stood there, with their usual giant smiles. Even though I had seen them many times over the years, it was kind of like a "love at first sight" moment. I was overjoyed and I immediately went over and hugged them both during the show.

I was thrilled to have crossed their paths once again. I think the fact that I was so happy to see them made me realize the value of their friendship in an instant. It meant something. As I was driving home, on the old Route 57, I kept thinking about how special these two "kids" were. The thought lingered for weeks. Then, I suddenly remembered a photo my good friend Bob Day posted on Facebook on our Class of 1971 site. It was a picture of Bob Sugar being the ref at one of the many kids' games he attended in one capacity or another. I searched the "Class of '71" page for the photo and I found it. It was one of the many photos that Bob Day so generously had taken and given away.

I happened to noticed a comment below by another classmate, Ted Palmitesso. It said, "Bob Sugar was probably one of nicest guys in our class. He's always been involved in activities involving kids. Very devoted to everyone and everything in his life." Ted nailed it.

Having graduated with Bob Sugar, I have known him for over 50 years and every time our paths crossed, he was always giving his time, or smile, away. Devoted was the perfect word as he was devoted to everyone he met or loved, especially to his bride of 50 years, Barb Young.

Barb Young Sugar is the same exact way. The first time I really got to know and appreciate this wonderful woman was when I was doing a "Show of Love" at the old St Paul's School. Barb was the principal of the now "Trinity Catholic School." Of course, that smile hit me like a ton of bricks, and anyone could see she absolutely loved those kids,

89

her staff and her job. Nobody was getting rich being the principal of a small Catholic school, but for Barb it clearly was a labor of love. She proved this when, after she retired, she continued to volunteer many hours to her favorite little school. Barb always carried such poise and grace as she interacted with the kids and her staff/friends and the parents.

Together now, for 50 years, Barb and Bob raised three children, Scott, Dave and Susan, and they are so blessed and grateful for their six wonderful grandkids. The truth is, I had run into these two "lovebirds" several times, most recently at "Porchfest" in Oswego. (They were holding hands.) This time when I saw them, something extra special happened. Perhaps, it was because I was pleasantly surprised when I turned quickly to find them there unexpectedly.

I love my Hometown of Oswego. It is truly is an exceptional place. One of the reasons it is so special is because of its people, model citizens like Robert and Barbara Sugar. They are the bedrock to this community. Our city and our world need more people like them. With the world going to hell and our country being more and more divided, these two prove there is still so much good around us. Just look at all these two have accomplished.

They have joined forces to do great things together, despite their vast differences. Afterall, they were from different sides of the river. Yes, both are from Oswego, but Bob was a "westsider" and Barb was an "eastsider." Yet, somehow, they managed to come together and do so much good. No matter our differences, we can all do this, no matter which side of the river we stand on.

I guess, to answer the question of why God put them together, it had to be fate. The only way to explain their destiny is that God had his hand it every step of the way. He knew what these two incredible individuals could do if paired together. The good these two have accomplished is immeasurable. Thank you, Barb and Bob and God.

The Man Who Would Not Smile

While performing shows at senior homes across the state, I have met some of the most interesting people and heard some of the most incredible stories. I would be lying if I told you I didn't see sadness. There's been plenty. Afterall, I am meeting these wonderful people at a time in their lives when, most likely, they are sick, sad or lonely. Many of them have recently lost a spouse or been forced to leave their life-long homes. They are in need of hope and happiness. I try to bring some.

I did meet one such man several years ago. His name was Vinnie. He was volunteering at a beautiful facility in Utica, New York called The Masonic Community. As I entered the activity area, a beautiful giant atrium, there was wonderful music coming from an elderly man over in a corner playing the piano. As I was setting up my equipment, I was enjoying this man's music. When it was time for me to start my one-hour performance, Vinnie simply pivoted around on his bench to watch the show.

I was taken back, as he clearly looked sad. It was not the expression I was expecting, on the face of the man who was just creating such happy and beautiful music. I locked in on that face. Before I started my performance, I introduced "The Man at The Keyboard" playing the wonderful music. The people

92

applauded; he did nothing. During the show I joked that I knew him, as we had spent several years in prison together. The audience roared; again, he didn't even crack a smile.

I continued my show and, at the conclusion, as they were wheeling most of the residents out, I noticed this sad man slowly approach me. I thought, here comes the man who just watched my entire show and never smiled once. Perhaps he was going to scold me? I was a tad nervous.

He reached out his hand like a gentleman and said, "Nice show, I'm Vinnie." With a sigh of relief I said, "I'm Joe." Before I could say my next words, he exhaled through pursed lips, as though he were trying to blow the sadness out of his chest. He said, "I just don't know, I just don't know." He began to share that he had received a "Not good" diagnosis. I immediately stopped what I was doing and invited Vinnie to come sit on the nearby bench to say what he, obviously, needed to get off his chest.

The sad conversation transpired. His wife was sick and a resident in that nursing home. He had been her caregiver for several years but at 85, he could no longer care for her at home. Vinnie visited her every day and he would play the piano for others while she slept. He had accepted that his wife of many years was sick and that he would always be there for her, but could not believe that he was now the sick one.

93

Frustration creeped in as he questioned how much longer he could care for her. The dignified man also threw in that he had a heart attack recently, as though it was just a cold. As he continued, he teared up and struggled to speak. He went silent. I just hugged him, hard. It was probably only a couple of seconds, but it was powerful. He leaned back and began to speak again, this time a bit softer. "You know I've been sick; my wife is sicker and I have already been struggling to keep up with her care and now, this."

He concluded with, "I've done my best. I've worked hard. I just don't know what's going to happen. I just wish God would give me some kind of sign that things are going to be okay." At the instant the words "Would give me some kind of sign" passed his lips, a leaf fell from the indoor tree and landed inside the collar of his shirt.

I was shocked at this sign from above and could not wait to hear Vinnie's reaction to this miracle. That's when he grabbed the leaf and threw it to the ground as though it were a pestering mosquito.

He didn't get it! He didn't see it! I jumped to my feet, threw my hands in the air and shouted: "Vinnie, you literally just asked God for a sign that things are going to be okay and a leaf falls, that very second, from an indoor tree, down your neck." I said,

"Vinnie, that's your sign!" He finally smiled and said, "I guess." I said, "Vinnie do you want to keep this leaf as a reminder of the Miracle?" He said, "Not really."

He finally smiled and I felt, at least briefly, I had given him a reprieve from his sorrows. There was really nothing left to say, so we hugged once more and I got on my way to the next show. I kept that leaf and it reminds of Vinnie a lot. How could he have not seen that sign? I realized that my most important job that day was simply point out to Vinnie that God was with him and he was not alone. I gave him a bit of hope.

I believe we all need to do this, as sometimes people are so sad, angry or scared they don't see the positive in the world. They don't recognize the good around us or the miracles that happen in their lives. We need to point it out especially to those who are alone in our nursing homes. On that day Vinnie smiled, and that's where love lives.

Do You Remember *The Waltons*?

Back in the 1970s, my favorite television show was *The Waltons*. It was a story about an (intergenerational) family all living under one roof together on a mountain top. The show centered around the eldest son, "John-Boy" Walton, growing up during the Depression era in rural Virginia. It was peaceful, comforting and always left you with a valuable lesson.

The show made a huge impact on me. So much so that, when I started raising my own family, I made it my mission to accumulate the entire collection of every episode on VHS tapes. We would sometimes watch them as a family, but my kids were "encouraged" to watch specific episodes as their punishment whenever they were grounded. I knew every episode by heart, therefore, I was able to customize the best show to address the specific transgression of that particular day.

There was no doubt that my family thought I was crazy when I announced my plan to drive 500 miles to Schuyler, Virginia to visit the actual Walton's Mountain. It was back in the mid- 1990s, when I felt compelled to visit the birthplace of the show's creator, Earl Hamner, and his family. This is where *The Waltons* show got its inspiration from. Call it impulsive or call it fulfilling destiny, but I needed to go there, and that I did.

In this little town in Nelson County, Virginia, in the Blue Ridge Mountains, you could see the original Walton homestead and actually visit the Walton's Museum. A substantial collection of memories and memorabilia was located in the former Hamner family school, located directly across the street from the house they all grew up in.

The annual grand opening of the museum was held in March, as it was closed during the winter. It was a big deal in this little museum as people (like me) would come from all over the country to see where it all began. It was a bigger deal as, on the grand opening, it was very likely that Earl Hamner himself, or actual members of the cast would make the journey home to visit this sacred ground. Well, as it turned out, I hit the jackpot. Earl Hamner was there, as well as other members of his family. A cast member, "Elizabeth Walton" (played by Kami Cotler) was in attendance too.

This is when the miracle happened. As they were getting prepared for the opening ceremony (where the guests of honor were to speak,) they had major technical difficulties with their PA System. I just happen to have one in the back of my truck. (The sound system I used for my "Show of Love" school programs). Needless to say, I saved the day for *The Waltons*.

After the ceremony I got the chance to speak personally with "John-Boy" (Mr. Hamner) himself. He thanked me. I told him of my occupation, traveling the Northeast teaching school kids "The Golden Rule." I shared with him that I watched every episode with my parents and kids. I thanked him for writing such a beautiful story showing how families should be.

His response surprised me when he said, "My goal wasn't to show how families should be, but to show how people should treat one another." The connection appeared and I realized my purpose for being there. He autographed my "Show of Love" sign and wished me luck in my "Future endeavors."

I brought that sign home and showed my dad. He was so proud! I then proceeded to take that sign on the road for a few more hundred school shows. It was meant to be and I felt destiny was fulfilled. As they would say, I've been to the mountain top. "Good night, John-Boy."

Best 1st Day of School, EVER

For over 35 years I have been performing school assembly programs, around New York State. I am still doing them, but only a handful since I am nearing retirement.

It's called "Show of Love." I know the name sounds funny and, believe me, I have taken a lot of heat over it. The name actually has been blocked from some school websites or emails because of love's possible meaning. I once had a principal request, as I entered the building, that I "Not use my sign (or the name) during the show."

It was at one of my many schools that I stumbled upon the greatest gift I had ever given. It was at a school just North of New York City, at a K-5 building. Like many times when I arrived at a school, I needed to check in at the office, sign in, get my picture taken and move on to set up my stuff. Well, this particular morning it was crazy busy, as it was the first day of school. I tried to get in and out of that office as quickly as possible to make the school secretary's job a little less hectic.

That's when first I noticed him, a young boy, sitting on the bench in the principal's office. Because of my frequent visits as a child, I could relate. I knew the look. He was scared and looked sad. I thought, oh no, someone's in trouble. I was using my power of observation, but the thing is …. I got it wrong.

His name was Rodrigo and that day was his first day, ever, at that school. He was transferring from another district and, evidently, his mom messed up on some paperwork. As the administrator and parent worked out the details, I had heard and seen enough to know that this terrified kid could use a little help.

Anyone who has seen one of my assemblies knows that my show teaches a lesson in caring and kindness. Just as important, I always include the audience, as I "randomly" pick kids to be the stars of the show. So, guess who was the star of the show that day? Rodrigo!

In that one-hour assembly I made him the focal point and the hero! In front of 550 of his new school/classmates, I gave him the best first day ever. I complimented his awesome shirt; I pointed out how much I liked his new glasses. I said, in front of everyone, what a cool kid he was. I was a "kingmaker" and I knew it. I used my superpowers to give this scared kid a leg up on one of his hardest days ever.

I have to believe it worked. I noticed as the kids were exiting the gym/show that day, his classmates were all over him. He was introduced, welcomed and accepted, all in one fell swoop. It was one of the most beautiful sights I had ever seen and one I will never forget. That was a gift that had immeasurable value.

In fact, the gift wasn't the show, or even making that kid a star. The real gift was merely taking a few seconds, in that main office that morning, to observe a kid in crisis and try to make it a little better. In a matter of just a few hours I transformed a frightened little boy into a huge smile with a little boy behind it.

The name "A Show of Love" was one I had given a lot of thought to. It was never meant to mean a show, like a performance. It was always meant to signify an action. A show of love was like an act of kindness or, in my case, a sign of faith.

"Envy the Working Man"
(Work is therapy)

Dad loved to work. He looked forward to going to work at the paper mill on Mitchell Street every single day of his career. He would say, with conviction, "I'm not afraid of dying, I'm only afraid of the day I can't work." Thank God, I got that from him, as I also found a job that I would love for over fifty years. These are stories of some of my fondest memories of my job, being an entertainer for the last fifty years.

Envy the working man

Where Were You on December 1st 1978?

Six Hundred friends, fans and followers were at the Woodshed Tavern in Oswego, New York on December 1st,1978. They were there in support of our local duo Side by Side. Paul Vandish and myself were desperate to record our first record. It was one heck of a fundraiser.

We were, of course, struggling musicians, having giving up our day jobs at Vona's Shoes and the Oswego Hospital. We had developed a great following and thought, if we threw a big party to say thank you to our loyal friends, we could raise a little cash to help pay for the record. It would be a win-win.

Enter Diane Broadwell, the owner of the Woodshed. She believed in us. She gave us our first job (now called gigs) and also graciously offered to host our party at her bar (now called Venues) to attempt our dream of throwing the biggest party ever in Oswego.

We had press releases in all the local papers, we had radio ads and posters plastered all over town, we had friends spreading the news by word of mouth. Most of all, we had faith it would happen, AND IT DID! Yes, over six hundred people packed that bar that night (to the rafters). We know this for a fact, as tickets were numbered and shown at the door.

The few kegs promised were gone in just over an hour. We sang, they danced and they drank (and drank). It was wild! We all had so much fun. Diane Broadwell bought a round for the packed bar. Incidentally, there were no fights, no gunshots and no stabbings that night, as no one ever lost respect for the establishment or their fellow patrons. Good thing, as our only security (bouncers) were our good friends Shirly Frake (RIP) and Joann Bateman who, with Diane, handled the onslaught of humanity that night.

I suppose we owe a debt of gratitude to the local police and fire departments, as they were gracious to look the other way when it came to fire code and parking violations.

Needless to say, we raised the money, we made the record and we fulfilled our dream, with a little help from our friends. The record had two original songs, "When She's Gone" and Hey Lady. To this day Paul and I remember and appreciate the kindness and generosity shown.

A huge and eternal thanks goes out to Diane, Joann, Shirley, Jennifer, Stephanie, The Woodshed Tabernacle Choir, The "Bones Crew" and our friends

from Oswego Hospital. (Especially Darlene & Patty.)
Last, but not least, thank you to the hundreds of
friends that showed up that night.

It's been nearly 50 years and we have not
forgotten it yet, we never will.

The Thanksgiving Day Miracle

There was a two-year window between when Paul Vandish and I first came together for the Jaycee Talent contest on March 1st 1976 and when we hit the road state wide with our duo, Side by Side.

During this time, Paul and I performed in Willow. The band was started by David (Skeets) Murabito and myself. Willow had a limited song list and very little success until Paul joined with his amazing voice. He also brought with him a style of music that people wanted to hear and dance to.

Paul and I would often go to the Great Laker Inn and watch the out-of-town bands like the Alligators, Crystal and The Wizz Kids pack the place. We dreamed of playing that room, but Carm (the owner) had a hard fast rule not to book local bands. Well, as it happened, on Thanksgiving night 1977, the out-of-town band canceled and Carm called us for our big chance. To be honest, the room was packed due to the advertised band, but when we played that night, we held that crowd and we rocked the place.

Needless to say, that launched our career in Oswego and propelled us statewide. Soon after, we got picked up by DMR talent agency out of Syracuse and we were on our way. We were a great '70s rock band.

109

Skeets, Willow's drummer, was one of the most talented musicians ever to come out of Oswego. John Readling was a great bass player. A little-known player joined us and shocked us with his amazing guitar ability. His name was Dave Sweet. He was a terrific guy. Paul Vandish was our ticket as he could play keyboards and that boy could sing. We traveled the state in the big blue Willow Bus and had the times of our lives!

I'll never forget the day my dad came home from his shift at Papertronics (the local paper mill) to find a full-size blue school bus in his driveway. He had to park in the yard, he walked toward me shaking his head and I thought for sure I was in trouble. When he reached me, he smiled and said, "I couldn't even afford a wheel barrow when I was your age and now my son owns a school bus." (He wasn't too happy when I told him I agreed to store it in our driveway.)

Though the band Willow only lasted for a short time those memories were some of the best ones of my life.

111

The Three Wooden Guitars

There have been a lot of vintage, high quality and expensive guitars that I have played, or run across, in my time growing up in Oswego, but none so important as the cheap plywood ones made by my dad back in the JTS Music days.

If you are from Oswego and you went to a wedding reception or a party back from 1980 till 2000, most likely you've seen one of these JTS wooden guitars in action. If you were one of the few, lucky, chosen ones, you may actually have played one of them.

I remember when my dad had the idea. At first, I thought it was a bit corny, but then he built them and his artist friend, Norm Beck, painted them and the rest, as they say, is history. Somehow, they always lit up the room.

I recently heard from my good friend Terry Schaffer and she reminded me that she actually owned one of those "collector items." It was one that Paul Vandish and I had given to her husband, and our good friend, Bodie back in the Side by Side days. There were only 12 made. I could never remember why I only had eleven left, now I know. It works out perfect as Denise and I have 11 grandkids so each one will have a Wooden Guitar left to them made by their Great Grampa. I know they will probably say; "What the heck are these?"

I do wonder, how many bridal parties have played in "the band" with those famous guitars? The Best Man and the Maid of Honor were always the leaders of the band and quite often a member of the bridal party would end up doing their guitar solo standing on top of our huge speaker. There were thousands of parties over those twenty years and so many wedding guest had fun playing like rock stars.

I know the value that these three guitars possessed based on the joy they created. Perhaps someday, if any of the bridal party's grandkids ever look at wedding pictures from way back in the 1980s and 1990s, they will know too. All they need to do is see the smiles on the faces of the bridal party playing those three wooden guitars. The chosen few who actually got to play a "Joe Trionfero original."

As my dad always said in the phrase he coined, "Love Lives in A Smile." He made those guitars... and those guitars made us smile.

Side by Side, Plays 21 Hour Gig, NON-STOP
September 1st 1980

If your old enough, you might remember The Jerry Lewis Muscular Dystrophy Telethon. It was a Labor Day tradition that was held from 1966 until 2010 (with Jerry Lewis and Ed McMahon).

This past New Year's Eve, I started thinking about Dick Clark and the Times Square celebration and then my mind immediately jumped to the MD Telethon, the other long-standing tradition of the '70s and '80s.

It was a huge deal where many of the most famous stars would perform throughout the night and many young people would try to stay up all night to witness and answer the challenge to help "Jerry's Kids."

Well, back in 1980, Side by Side answered that challenge in a big way. Paul Vandish and myself donated our services to the local MD affiliate to try to support the good cause. While doing so, we would also attempt to set the record for the longest, nonstop, live performance. This marathon show would last 21 (and a half) hours and be held at the very popular night spot, Club 37 in North Syracuse.

Paul and I played and sang all day and all night, as a few dozen brave souls (dressed in athletic wear and pajamas) literally danced the night away. All the local news outlets covered it and, of course, it was a huge success and raised a ton of money.

I have to admit, it was fun the first 5 or 6 hours, but it got real around 6:00 AM the next morning and we still had another 12 hours to go. It was hard back then but my 72-year-old self can't even fathom doing it now. We did it and we survived, but not without a hitch. While performing through the long night someone stole my gear and clothes stored behind the stage (including my guitar case). Human nature sure is funny. Despite this, it was a truly great memory. Love was in the room that long night in September of 1980.

"The Million Dollar Quartet"
Derrick Coleman, Sherman Douglas, Stevie Thompson and Howard Triche

During my five decades of performing, I have stumbled across some pretty amazing opportunities. I believe one of the greatest was on December 6th of 1986.

I only know the exact date because, for the past 40 years, on the first Saturday of December, I have performed for the annual Kid's Christmas Party for the Upstate Hospital (Now Golisano's Children's Hospital) in Syracuse, New York. It was during the JTS Music years and, just like all of the other thousands of parties I did, my goal was to get the audience involved and to have fun.

What I didn't plan on that day was who would be in the audience. Because the party was being held on one of the floors in the hospital, in the vicinity of "The Hill," the Syracuse Men's Basketball Team was able to pop over to greet the kids and sign some autographs. At the conclusion of their session, I sprang into action.

I just happened to have with me the JTS Music wooden guitars, (my dad had made,) a saxophone and some drumsticks. Just as Roger Springfield (sports director @ WSTM) was shuffling the players off to their next stop, I commandeered the team before they got to the exit. Before they knew what hit them, I had instruments in their hands, microphones in front of them and the first few notes of "Old Time Rock and Roll" playing.

Because of the spontaneity of the situation, and being caught off guard, they didn't have time to resist. They jumped right in, played along and that room exploded! The kids went crazy, as did the organizers and any medical staff who were within earshot of this phenomenon. I had caught lightning in a bottle for those kids and they were ecstatic.

Obviously, it was a huge hit with everybody, and for one brief moment, those legends were "Rock Stars" instead of Basketball Stars. Yep, I can say I played with Derrick and the Dominators.; (The name I gave them) In the picture below you will see the "Million Dollar Quartet" and me. I'm the short guy.

Turns out, Love does Lives in a Smile. If you don't believe me, you would have if you'd seen the smiles on those kids' faces.

119

Touring with Grampa

I have eleven grandkids and every one of them grew up "touring" with Grampa during summer breaks and holidays. They traveled to hundreds of senior homes across New York, performing a variety of fun shows.

It became a rite of passage to get one of the coveted seats in Grampa's van. I was not babysitting and they were not just roadies. They sang, danced, told jokes, and read speeches. They were hugged hundreds of times (willingly) by thousands of seniors. Most important, the kids listened to the seniors' stories, lessons and memories of times long past. No phones were allowed. They learned citizenship and decency from a generation that knew how to treat each other. It was a match made in Heaven: my grandkids and the "Greatest Generation."

For the most part, they have pretty much all grown up now. The oldest is 30 and the youngest is 14. I still, occasionally, hear them refer back to a story that they remembered from the road touring with Grampa.

At 72, I continue to perform shows at senior homes all around New York. (Including Oswego and the greater Syracuse area.) My oldest and youngest grandsons, Ben & Theo, still travel with me and it makes me so proud when they share the show/stage with me. They might even consider taking over the business some day when I stop performing. Nothing would make me happier.

How lucky was I, to have been able to share those precious years and collect all those priceless memories with my grandkids. There was no greater gift.

My 1st Band My 1st Story

Last November 20th (2024), I ran across an old song list from my very first band. It was started back the 1960s. We called ourselves The C.R.O.P. (Citizens Restoration of Peace.) This was long before my Side by Side days with Paul Vandish. We may have been the first "garage band" since we played more in my garage than we ever did anywhere else.

It consisted of Ray Furniss, (RIP) Tommy Navagh and myself. (It actually was started by my cousin Ralph Mclaughlin.) Tommy was a gifted bass player from a very young age and such an easy-going guy. Ray could certainly play that Guild guitar, but what I remember most was his amazing voice. What a sweet voice it was. Ray was a terrific person and one of Oswego's finest. He was taken way too soon. He is still remembered and missed.

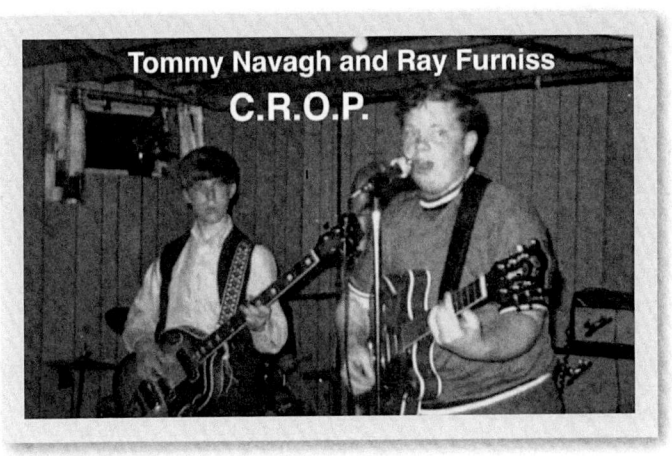

Tommy Navagh and Ray Furniss
C.R.O.P.

Four T-Shirts Define My Entire Career

Early one morning it dawned on me that my entire life (career) could be summed up in just four T-shirts. Any musician knows what I am talking about. Before it was called "Merch" they were just called "band T-shirts." The reason I remembered them at all is I have one hanging on my wall. It was one my dad actually had made for the Show of Love.

My Dad always wore my "band T-shirts." He was so proud of my music career he wore those shirts all the time. He had my complete collection saved in a box that we found while going through some of his things a few years back. I was so proud that they mattered that much to him. I dug them out of my basement and began to reminisce.

Okay, full discloser, the first shirt of my career wasn't a "band shirt" at all. My first job ever was working at Vona Shoes for my first, best and only boss Zeke (Francis) Vona. I was able to work full time (36 hours a week) due to the split sessions at OHS for my entire 11th and 12th year. This Vona Shoes T-shirt was from a basketball team I started with Dick (Sheigs) Gill and Bodie Schaffer. I left the shoe business for the show business in the mid 1970s to pursue my dream of playing in a band. Then for the next 50 years, I added just three more T-shirts. Those shirts were, pretty much, the story of my life.

Side by Side, JTS Music and Show of Love.

I decided I am going to keep my four shirts and use them as a resume for when I go looking for my next job. Who knows maybe Larry Trenca will hire me for his next band.

"Thirst for Knowledge"
(Did you learn anything?)

From the time we were old enough to understand, our father would rarely yell at us. Instead, his go-to phrase was always, "Did you learn anything." Dad loved to learn and had a reverence for knowledge. He would refer to it as an "Edjamacation." These stories are some of the profound lessons I have learned from him and his lawn mowers.

Did you learn anything?

"Do The Right Thing"

Back in the 1960s I remember sitting around the dinner table, every night, with my family and we would talk. Yes, talk. We would discuss our days at work or school, current events of the day or the status of family and friends. Every now and then, when school did come up, we would, "discuss" our expected behavior. It was short and sweet. Our dad would always simply say, "Do the right thing." If it was really important, he would remind us of our last name and warned us to do right by that "Trionfero" name, as it was the most valuable thing we had.

For the most part, we were pretty good, although, my being hyper active certainly got me into trouble, due to my lack of impulse control. At school or home, we kids knew what was expected of us when it came to being responsible and making good choices. I remember when we did slip up and began to offer an excuse, it was often met with my mom's instant reply, "Coulda Shoulda Woulda." Things we could do and shouldn't, things we should do and don't, and things we would do… if we were responsible. There were no acceptable excuses.

Mom taught us, all day, every day, that doing the right thing was important. Our number one lesson was you couldn't be kind of responsible. You either were or weren't. She once taught me the most powerful lesson when she reminded me, "Once you cross the line between right and wrong it disappears and, because you can no longer see it, you drift further and further away from doing the right thing."

Now in my seventies, I find myself reflecting, a lot, about that dinner table on Fifth Street Road and wonder what my parents would think of the world today. I can see them shaking their heads. There is so much selfishness and greed. So many people being, "kind of responsible." Good citizens are getting harder and harder to come by. Responsibility has slowly deteriorated over the decades.

The best example I can give is driving on our crazy roadways today. I remember when my parents taught us how to drive, we stopped at a caution light. When we taught our kids to drive, it was okay to go through that caution light. Now our grandkids are driving and they are speeding up to make that it through that caution light. One of them even said, "Red means stop, green means go and yellow means go like hell to beat the red." The truth is, today, unless there are traffic cams at the intersection, some people never even stop.

You see, we are all part of the problem. All of us, "fudge a bit." We do 70 mph in a 65 zone. We glance at out phones for "just a second" and we sometimes make that right turn on red, even if that sign says not to. They are just small infractions, but, as my mom would remind us, the line has disappeared.

129

The bottom line is, if we are not part of the solution, then we are part of the problem. The beauty of responsibility is that we get two chances at it. First, we can do the right thing or, second, when we do the wrong thing, we can admit it and correct it. It seems so easy, but admitting it is so hard.

I am reminded of a quote that one of my dad's old bosses, Lew Irwin, use to say, "Never do that, which if everyone did, would ruin society." As for me, I am going to remember what my mom told me about that line between right and wrong disappearing.

I am also going to remember what her mom (My Gram) always said, "The worlds' going to hell in a handbasket." I say, let us all take a breath and remember that scary, but true, statement that we all heard as kids; "Give the devil an inch and he'll take a mile." We can do better. We owe it to our kids.

Where Did You Learn How to Drive?

Funny you should ask. One day, when I was on the road (again), as I was pumping gas at the local "mini-mart in Waverly, New York, a young gunner come whipping through the crowded parking lot. A guy who had hair like me (it was grey) shouted, to no avail, "Where did you learn how to drive?" It immediately brought me back to the 1960s, and my two heroes who taught me to drive, my Driver Ed. teacher, Mr. Frank Bartello, and my dad, Joe Trionfero.

Both were patient and kind men; each being even keeled and good tempered. They were both good drivers and good citizens. On the two-hour drive home that day, I had a lot of time to reflect on the terrible state of drivers on the roads these days. I thought, how many gatherings of families and friends begin these days with the latest, "Bad driver of the day" story or the close call recently encountered.

Rightfully so, everyone is complaining, but it's not making it any better, at all! I smiled as I remembered a Thanksgiving back in the '80s when my mom and dad came to our house in Baldwinsville for dinner. As they entered our kitchen, my mom was spitting nails as she complained about a close call they had with an "idiot driver" on the road during their trip, "Over the river and through the woods."

She was mad as heck and she even used a swear word. My dad, on the other hand, was calm and collected. I asked, "What happened, Dad?" Before he could answer, my mom shouted out, "Nothing. All he did was the Sign of The Cross." My dad finally spoke and said softly, "I saw no sense in yelling at him, so I said a prayer for his safety instead, as he obviously could use it."

I think about that a lot these days. I see so many people flippin' and, cuttin' each other off, complaining and retaliating. I thought about it and I have come up with the four most important lessons I learned about driving that I'd like to pass on to the next generations. One from each of my teachers, one from my, then, 16-year-old daughter Dacey and one from a street sign in Chenango Bridge, New York, (across from an elementary school I was working at).

1. Mr. Bartello taught me to be a good citizen behind the wheel. He would say, "Treat other drivers the way you would want them to treat you."
2. My dad would say, "When you are driving, you can only be mad at the mistakes you've never made before." He also said, "Don't take it out on the car and always leave yourself enough time."
3. My daughter, Dacey, shocked me one time with her response to my lesson. I said, "You have to be careful, 50% of the drivers on the road are jerks." She come back immediately, saying, "Dad, don't

you mean everyone on the road is a jerk 50% of the time?"

4. The sign on the banks of the Chenango River, across from the school, simply says, "Drive as though it was your child was at play here." Wow, empathy. What a concept.

It all comes down to putting ourselves in other people's shoes. Empathy, kindness and compassion. The same things Mr. Bartello and Dad taught and the same lessons we have all learned from someone we respected or loved.

I'll leave you with one parting thought. It was something that Dorothy, a resident at a Senior Home in Horseheads, said as I was packing up to go. "Be careful driving home. Never drive faster than your angels can fly." Between shows one day, my Grandson Ben (Goodsell) and I were discussing "driving distracted." With the help of google and a calculator we made an alarming discovery. Consider this:

1. If the car you're driving is going 60 MPH you would be **traveling one mile per minute.**

2. Because there are 5280 feet in a mile you are **traveling 5280 feet in one minute.**

3. If you are traveling 5280 feet per min you are **traveling 88 feet per second.**

4. A regulation **NBA basketball court is 94 feet long.**
5. Therefore, when you are driving 60 mph, for every second you glance at your phone, you are traveling almost the full length of an NBA court. EVERY SECOND you travel THAT FAR **blindfolded.**

Please consider this before the next time you "glance" at your phone for "just a second or two." Be safe.

Capisce?

As a young child, in Oswego, New York in the 1950s, my first word that I really understood from our Italian dad was, "Capisce." As a young kid, I am pretty sure I didn't speak Italian, however, the tone and inflection helped me to comprehend the meaning. It's kind of funny that the first word that I truly understood literally meant to understand. However, my first real important lesson in life was from my mom when she taught me to "Put Yourself in Their Shoes."

This all came together in the Summer of 1958. It was just before I started kindergarten at School # 2 on Mitchell Street in Oswego. What I remember was getting into big trouble, as I stole my best friend's brand-new toy gun. To make matters worse, I then buried it in the alley between our houses on E. Schuyler Street. I remember, vividly, being caught and taught one of my most valuable lessons of my life.

I knew I was in trouble, as my mom had promised (warned) me, "You wait till your dad gets home." The minute my dad got home from work, "the lesson" began. Even though we waited all day, in anticipation, for the "enforcer" to come home it was still my mom who spoke first. She began to tell me how wrong it was and, of course, I felt bad. Even at five, I knew it was wrong.

Afterall, that's why I hid the stolen toy. But it's what she said next that got to me, even as a little boy. My mom proceeded to remind me of the fire that our neighbor's family had experienced recently and that they had lost most of their belongings, including all of my friend's toy. The toy gun I stole, and hid, was his only toy. I was old enough to feel terrible.

My mom had just taught me a lesson in empathy. She closed with her go-to phrase, "Put yourself in their shoes." My dad punctuated that saying with "Capisce?" My mom was telling me I should try to understand my neighbor and my dad was telling me I'd better understand my mom. To this day, although I do not remember the punishment, I do remember the lesson.

Ironically, this all came to mind as I was performing one of my "Show of Love" programs at Northside Elementary School in Fairport New York. The presentation's title was, of course, "Put Yourself in Their Shoes." I draw much comfort teaching students that same lesson that my mom taught me over 65 years ago.

Those words still rang true, but now I was now the teacher explaining to hundreds of kids what I had learned so long ago. We all know the golden rule; even a 5-year-old knows it. "Treat people the way you want to be treated." However, it's EMPATHY which activates to the golden rule. Once we understand what someone feels and why they feel it, we change our behavior and the way we treat them. We become kinder and more caring people.

We all need to be reminded of this lesson as the world, as my Gram would say, is going to hell in a handbasket. We can do better. All it takes is just a couple of extra seconds to try to understand what the other person is going through.
Thanks Mom & Dad

The Great Snowball War of 65

Way back in the winter of '65 we Kingsford Park students carried on a long-standing tradition of going out on lunch recess and looking to throw some snowballs at those St. John's kids. The two schools were only a block apart, so we both staked our claim to this very small neighborhood on the west side of Oswego. If the snow was good packing and the weather was nice, then a "war" was likely that day.

Well, the conditions were ripe on a great day in February that year. (I only remember because it was close to Valentine's Day.) We knew, early that morning, that day would be the big one. As soon as we got outside for lunch, we lined up our armies on each side of Niagara Street and began pelting snow balls.

The epic battle didn't really last that long, as a few cars interrupted the barrage of snowballs. I do remember hitting someone in the face and feeling bad about it. Even at a young age, I thought what a stupid tradition, and why, on earth, did it continue? This same type of rivalry carried over into our CYO basketball games when we St. Joe's kids played against the St. John's kids; they always beat us.

Fast forward 50 years and some of those St. John "MONSTERS" turned out to be some of my really good friends. Bodie Schaffer, Don Conisky, Gigsy Enwright and John Hall, just to name a few. Two of my closest friends, Tom Price and Paul Vandish, actually lived in the St John's "hood."

The lesson I learned…. The bigger my world got, the more I realized how close we all could have (and should have) been. First, when I became a high school student, I started playing baseball and basketball with Bodie and some of these St. John boys, I surprisingly saw them for the good kids they were and it began to change my perspective.

When I got older, I started to see myself as an Oswegonian, not just a "west sider." I began to work side by side with some of the same young men I was so afraid of as a kid. Of course, many of these former "enemies" became friends as I crossed paths with them often in our little hometown.

Before I turned thirty, I moved to Baldwinsville and became a resident of Central New York. At the same time, I also began to travel the state for my job. There would be times those St. John's kid names would pop up. I was quite proud to claim them as friends, as they too were from Oswego, New York. It felt so good just to say their names out loud. The bigger my world got, the more these people mattered to me. How silly that childhood prejudice seemed.

You see, the truth is, we are not just members of a small neighborhood on the west side of Oswego. We are citizens of a small world that continues to shrink at an incredible rate. The older I got, the more I realized we have to share this world with all of our fellow earthlings.

It turns out it's a small world after all. It took my world getting bigger to realize how small it really was. The smaller it got, the closer I felt to others. My ability to relate and empathize grew. My dad and mom (Joe & Inez) taught us, from an early age, regardless of our differences, to treat EVERYONE the way that we would want to be treated. How did they get to be so smart?

My Greatest Business Idea
(That Failed Miserably)

Back in the mid 1980s, when I was in my mid-thirties, I was thinking a lot about my grandparents that I never met. My dad's parents were straight out of Italy and both passed away, within days of each other, just before my first birthday.

To be honest, the initial thought of them came at my doctor's office when I was being asked about my medical history, but their memory lingered on the drive home. Over the next few days, they would randomly pop into my head. Who were they, what were they like and am I anything like them? I would have given a million dollars just to sit down with them for an hour. I had so many questions. I thought quickly of how lucky my kids were to get to know their grandparents and how I hoped that even some of my grandkids might be fortunate enough to someday look back and remember my parents as well. Then the idea hit, they could.

Right around the same time, in the mid 1980s something else happened…. video camcorders. Video cameras were introduced in the early part of that decade. The Sony Betacam burst on the scene in 1982. However, it wasn't until the mid-eighties that personal camcorders became portable, accessible and affordable. My wheels started to turn. Sure, video cameras would be great at documenting special events like weddings, school plays and recitals but, I thought, their absolute best use would be in capturing the images, stories and personalities of our family elders.

Technology finally afforded us the opportunity to preserve family history on tape. How great it would be if we could offer our children and grandchildren the opportunity to see, and get to know their grandparents or even great-grandparents. Video Time Capsules was born.

I would videotape interviews of my parents, my grandmother and my aunt and uncle. I would record for posterity their stories and personalities with a little bit of history on the side. (Not even to mention the genealogy aspect.)

Being an entertainer helped interviewing skills and I could use one of my brother Marshall's camcorders that he had purchased for his Video business, JTS Video. I thought it was more than a great idea, it was a business model that I could expand and offer the same priceless service to anyone who, like me, wished to capture these memories.

We had the cameras, the necessary lighting and microphones. Now all we needed to do was practice and then when we were ready hit Central New York with an advertising blitz. I proceeded to set up and perform practice interviews, for free, with family members, close friends and neighbors to hone in my interviewing skills. I did my family first then I did about a half of dozen for friends to get used to questioning people I did not know. I read books, watched other interviews and, in a few short weeks, felt ready to launch the greatest business idea ever.

After some thought and research, I decided the best approach would be to target the advertising to everyone, as anyone was a potential customer. Although I did feel I was offering a valuable service, I envisioned it as a huge money maker too. The profits were going to be huge. I decided on a price of $200 which would include a two-hour interview, a photo collage of their favorite pictures and 4 copies (tapes) of the final product. There would be no obligation to buy; basically, it was a free trial with nothing to lose.

I contacted the Post Standard, the Syracuse daily paper, and purchased an insert to be placed in every single one of their thousands of Sunday Papers, called the "Herald American." It cost me $975, a lot of money in 1987, but thousands of families would receive my bright pink flier. All I had to do was have the staff on hand to answer calls, schedule times to start interviews and get ready to count the money.

Monday morning came and, as I sat in my office with my staff at our JTS building staring at the phones, nothing happened. The phone did not ring. We did not receive one call. Not one. There were no interviews to schedule and I was bewildered. To this day I will never understand how others, like me, could not see the value in capturing the memories of our loved ones for future generations. Was it the price? Was the concept too new? I'll never really know since I threw in the towel, cut my losses and focused on my next idea.

Looking back now I wonder, perhaps it was just not meant to be. Maybe it was because God had a bigger plan in store for me. It was only months later I would launch my "Show of Love" assembly program and, it would be a huge success.

I am very grateful for my accomplishments and successes I have had in my life but, to this day, I remain a bit miffed. I feel the "Video Time Capsule" idea was my best and most important Idea I ever had and it failed terribly. But what I do have are videotaped interviews of my parents, grandmother and my aunt and uncle preserved, "in the cloud," for all future generations to see…. and "that's not nothing." In fact, it really is everything.

09.16.87

The Squirrel that Taught me a Lesson
(The Story of "Spot")

I hate squirrels. I guess it would be more accurate to say that I love birds so much that the little grey creatures are a nothing but a nuisance. However, I must confess, there is one squirrel I have grown a fondness for and an attachment to. His name is "Spot." Yep, I named him. Let me explain. It all started Christmas of 2022, when my daughter in-law, Lori, gave me a birdfeeder.

I loved it! I hung it on an old dog run (line) that I never used, but left it up just in case. I got a lot of cool birds very quickly. Being a little hyper, I really enjoyed watching the birds hanging out at my feeder. It calmed me down and brought me peace. I added a couple more different types of feeders. It was glorious, but then the squirrels arrived. Several of them. They would all gather on the ground under the feeders eating the dropped food.

I wasn't crazy about the extra mouths to feed, but it was okay, as long as they stayed on the ground. Where I drew the line was when they started making the 6 ft jump to the feeder from the wall on the edge of our patio. The first time I saw them do it I was really angry. Whether or not they knew it, we were going to war.

I outsmarted the "herd" and put a six-inch piece of metal flashing on top of the wall to stop them. It worked, but they started to make the seven-foot jump from the metal can on the patio holding the feed. Well, I moved that can and relaxed again until I witnessed what I thought was, the impossible. They started scaling the 40-foot line to get to the feeder. I actually smiled a bit as I realized I had to ratchet up my game.

I was going to defeat them no matter what. I used plastic Coke and milk bottles around the line. They persevered. I then thought to use round foam pipe insulation as it would roll like a barrel. There was no way they could stand on that. They crawled underneath the line! Finally, I greased and oiled the entire line including the bottles and guess what? They started from the other side, ran across the top of the bottles, barely skimming the surface, and leaped to the prize. "They" still got to the feeders. I resigned myself to the fact that "these" squirrels had won. I had no more tricks, I was defeated.

I was just about ready to remove the feeders when something amazing happened. I noticed a white "spot" on the left shoulder of the culprit. I stopped and realized that it was the same spotted squirrel that I was seeing, every time. This was not a group of them at all; it was only one damn squirrel. I stopped for a moment and talked to myself, (yeah, he had me talking to myself) I said, "Out of the dozens of squirrels in this neighborhood, how is it that only this one could beat me."

Just for a moment I allowed myself to marvel at his skill. He had shown so much persistence, determination and bravery and, yeah, he was a bit crazy! I literally said to myself this squirrel can, and will, do anything necessary to succeed or survive.

Then something clicked in my mind. I stopped and thought back forty years ago, when that grey "fox" was me when I was struggling to get my new business (JTS) off the ground. That spotted creature had displayed the same characteristics I needed and used to succeed and survive back in the mid 1980s. Something had changed for sure. I started to respect him.

I rewarded him with a name "Spot," and a lifetime supply of unlimited bird food. Well, one thing led to another. He started to coming to the kitchen window when I was washing the dishes. I am not sure if he was thanking me or taunting me, but either way, we bonded.

Yes, something special happened to me that day. God sent me a squirrel to teach me a lesson. You see, at the moment I noticed that spot on his shoulder, I realized it was not just A squirrel…. it was THE squirrel. The one with the smarts, determination and bravery. I saw him for what he was and the attributes he possessed. He wasn't just part of a "herd." My prejudice against that rodent had faded away. That little guy changed the way I thought.

The next time I start to judge someone, I will look for their "spot" first, their unique gifts they possess.

Sure, I have a lot of cool birds, just like lots of people, but only I have an amazing, spotted squirrel that puts a smile on my face every time I see him. He is different, unique and special!

To answer your obvious question, YES, my wife and kids (and brothers & sister) do think I'm crazy, and probably some of my neighbors too. It's okay, because I love that squirrel, he makes me smile and….. That's where love lives.

Nobody Says "I Love You" Anymore

I received a nice emoji the other day. I think it had a smile or perhaps it was a heart… no wait, I think it was a pair of brown socks or maybe a spatula. I guess in the grand scheme of things, I don't really remember what it was.

I am not sure who sent it, and to be perfectly honest, I don't know if I even care. If that person had stopped by to see me for a visit or even taken a minute for a quick call, I am sure I would have remembered it and it would have mattered more. These days, nobody connects or really says how they feel.

Somewhere along the line, caring became like a forgotten language. People just don't express it like they used to or perhaps they just don't feel it. I get "E" Cards for my special days and an occasional email that's not junk mail, where someone is actually trying to convey a sentiment to me. I do get texts, of course I do. I have five kids and eleven grandkids. I get lots of texts, and I get emojis.

I understand, I really do. People are so busy these days with work and school being so important. Yeah, I get that. Don't get me wrong, I absolutely love hearing from my family. Anyway, they want to communicate is fine, but oh how I wish for that phone call or visit. Truth is, I just want to have a conversation. Yes, I miss the human contact. What I miss the most is…… an "I love You." Nobody says it anymore. When someone dares to say it these days it's almost always the safer, "Love Ya." (Often accompanied with a couple pats on the back.) Somewhere along the way, "I Love You" got a bad rap and was banished to the scrap heap along with "God Bless You."

I know a lot of us blame the kids and their cell phones for this, but this disconnect was started by us a long time ago and it just grew exponentially. I believe we started this whole avalanche with the snowball we created called the answering machine. Think about this: It was the first time that we could avoid a conversation with someone we loved by leaving a message instead. The "one-way conversation" was born.

I am truly ashamed of myself as I sadly recall a time when I was calling my parents' house and I was relieved to get my mom's answering machine so I could just leave a message. I just didn't have the time to talk. What I wouldn't give for those few minutes right now, for one last conversation.

No one is innocent here. We are all part of the problem, so we should all be part of the solution. We can do better! Stop by for a quick visit or use that phone, already in your hand, to make a call, instead of a text. Take the time to connect…. even if it's for just a minute. We are losing the ability to connect. Like the old AT&T commercial said, "Reach out and touch someone," for real. It makes a difference.

Connecting The Generations

I think we can all agree that the world is in trouble as we collectively worry about our grandkids' future and the next generation. Although I don't recommend it, all you need to do is turn on the news to see a country divided and a planet in peril. I have the answer. It's not as much that I have it, but I do know where to find it: it's with the Greatest Generation.

These heroes saved the world once before and, with our help, they can do it again. I am old enough to remember the greatness of my parents and grandparents. If you are a baby boomer, like me, then consider yourself fortunate to be members of the luckiest generation. Having been raised by those stellar citizens we were able to witness, first-hand, a level of civility and kindness that has become so difficult to find these days.

We watched an entire generation of elders display an earnest work ethic combined with a profound dedication to respect and responsibility. Our generation did okay, but our most important job is still before us. We must make sure that the next generation receives the insight and wisdom that the last generation entrusted to us. So, where do we find these legends that possess the keys to knowledge and understanding? Sadly, many of them are in our nursing homes. Truth be told, it's we boomers who are now aging out and starting to enter some of these very same facilities. Time is of the essence!

I am a father of five (adult) children with a collection of eleven older grandkids. Twenty years ago, I had an epiphany. Realizing that the world was going to hell, I decided to do something about it. Of course, I tried my best to be a good role model knowing full well I couldn't hold a candle to my parents' generation. This is when I decided to go one step further and take my show (and grandkids) on the road.

At the time, I had already presented my school program, (The Show of Love) thousands of times and decided to design a show just for senior citizens. This would allow them to become the conduit between the generations by passing on the wisdom they had learned from their parents before them to the kids of today (especially my grandkids).

It was not long into this journey I realized that the vast wisdom of these seniors often manifested itself in the form of old sayings and adages. They would share these with my grandkids, just like my parents did with me. I played into their strength designing questions my grandkids could ask them that would invite these pearls of wisdom during our one-hour shows.

Over and over again, my kids would hear the same advice that had been passed down for generations. We all know them; "Treat people the way you want to be treated." "If you can't say anything nice, don't say anything at all." And, of course, "If all your friends jumped off the bridge...." These are just a few of the classics that are seared into our conscious minds by those who we revered so much. The greatest generation is rapidly passing on now, leaving us, their children, with the formidable task of trying to turn the tide of this wave of selfish indifference and indulgence. Sure, we should remember and repeat these mantras at every teachable moment. More important, we should live these lessons and teach our grandkids by practicing what we preach. We must never forget the paramount importance of "Actions speak louder than words."

This is no easy task living in our divided country. These timeless lessons are even harder to teach in times of such fear and anger. We all proclaim, "It's not me, it's them," but the truth is.... we all can do better. Whether we like it or not, our actions and words our constantly being quietly observed by our grandkids.

I always remember the two sayings that my mom and dad repeated so many times. They seem so important today. "Don't judge another person until you walk a mile in their shoes" and "Two wrongs don't make a right." Last, but not least, our parents continually reminded us of the one saying we had heard so many times from our church; "Do unto others as you would have others do unto you."

It's been 25 years now and I have watched most of my grandkids grow up and learn from the Greatest Generation. These "kids" are all older now, ranging in ages between 14 and 30. In fact, my oldest grandson, Ben, still performs with me, but now its him asking the seniors for advice. How lucky they were to have had the benefit of all that extra wisdom and how grateful I am to have had access to that wonderful reservoir of knowledge and decency. It's as though my grandkids had hundreds of grandparents.

I think we all know that if we are going to save this world and re-unite our country, we must truly learn to love one another. It is imperative we remember the one ominous lesson we also learned as children: "United We Stand, Divided We Fall."

The Greatest Generation did teach us right from wrong. Let us turn their words into our actions. Let us not allow our fear or anger, or even a political identity, to erase our parents' teachings or Christian beliefs. Our parents deserve it and they would expect nothing less from us. We can save the world again, just by remembering what our parents taught us and passing it down to the next generations.

The Pledge They Take
"Is the one we break"

On March 28th, 2025, I did my last school show of the year at Pal Mac high school for middle school students. As I was setting up before the presentation, I began to reflect on my career and the 4300 school shows I had done over the past 35 years. My mission was simply to stop the hurt. I reflected on where our country was heading and I sadly thought about the numerous signs displayed on the walls of our kids' schools. Those sacred messages that we teach are kids and our parents taught us like: "Be Kind," "Respect" and of course, "Treat People the Way You Want to be Treated." If only we could.

I then heard the "Pledge of Allegiance" from the morning announcements. There it was, that solemn promise we have all said so many times in our lives. The phrase that kept sticking in my craw was, "One nation under God… indivisible." I thought, where in the world did, we go wrong. It certainly did not feel like one nation, at all.

We now live in a divided country where a kind of tribal mentality is taking hold, as everyone blames the other side for the problems in their homes and in their nation. One thing I know for sure, it's not the kids' fault, it's ours, the adults, and it is high time for us to practice what we preach. A few minutes later, I began my show that I had done so many times before, but this time it was different. Even though I was standing in front of an auditorium full of students, I was really addressing the millions of Americans in our fractured "United" States.

I thought, enough of the hypocrisy. It's time for all of us to come together and teach our children, by example, how to respect others and peacefully co-exist. The "Do as I say, not as I do" era has come to an end. Our kids are smart and painfully very observant.

I began: "Everyone knows the golden rule but, the truth is it's broken every day." The secret to the golden rule is in my show's title: Put Yourself in Their Shoes. I believe what's wrong with our world today is a lack of empathy and the solution is improving our ability to feel what others are feeling. Empathy is, in fact, the activator to the golden rule. Understanding others does not come easy for a human race that is genetically hard-wired to focus on self- preservation. Selfishness comes naturally to us.

The method I chose to accomplish this lofty goal of teaching empathy was to teach the students to develop a skill-set that allows them to become better listeners. The lesson, listening with our ears, eyes and heart to find out what someone else feels. In a society where no one really listens to each other anymore the answer is simple and profound.

Listening with our ears: We can truly hear what others are feeling but how, in Heaven's name, can we identify emotions when we are always listening to something else. We can't hear what others are feeling unless we take the headset off, the earbuds out, turn the device down and the TV off. This will allow us to focus and really listen. We must tune out noise. We live in a time where there is a constant distraction twenty-four hours a day.

Listening with our eyes: As crazy as it sounds, we forget that we can actually see what someone is feeling. Sure, it's about reading body language, but there is more. Making eye contact is essential for any real connection or relationship. My gram would always say, "The eyes are the window to the soul." I am a true believer that you can look into someone's eyes and see what's in their heart. The problem today is our obsession with the tiny screens in our hands. Think about this.

Back in the olden days we would focus on the people in our presence and one in a while, look up to the screen. Today, we are all primarily focused on the screen and once in a while we look up to the people in our presence. If we are truly going to connect, we must put the devices away and re-learn how to connect and make eye contact.

Listening with our heart: We must slow down. We live in a time where everyone strives to be first and fast. As a culture we have become programed to respond to the need for speed. Microwave ovens, Stop & Go convenience stores and, of course, megabytes per second are just a few examples. We have also trained generations of kids to respond quickly by standing over them and counting to three in order to get them to comply or complete a task. Time is of the essence! The problem with this? If you really want to teach your children to understand others, you have to teach them to take their time and to listen slowly, thus, "Listening with our heart."

I am well aware of the task before me and the level of difficulty to accomplish it. I do get discouraged from time to time but never deterred as I witness the epidemic of meanness and the division that exist in our country today. I am old, and wise enough to know everything is at stake. I am certain the solution begins with putting the cell phones down and engaging with others. The old phrase, "If left to our own devices," has taken on a whole new meaning. It's time to show our kids how to treat others as our actions do speak louder than our words.

I believe we have reached a tipping point. The moment in time that will make or break us, as a civilization. We must all act now, as both the reason and the answer stand right before us, our children. The solution lies within those first two words that we teach our kids, that our parents taught us, "BE NICE." Sadly, some may ask; who should we be nice to or, worse yet, who can we exclude from our kindness? My mind drifts back once again to the pledge they make and the one we break. It always ends the same, With Liberty and Justice for ALL. It's the reason I started the "Show of Love" in the first place. We all must teach and follow that simple rule, we all learned as kids, "Treat people the way you want to be treated."

"God, I Love It"
(Revel in the good stuff)

Whenever our dad faced adversity he would remain strong and determined and almost shout, "Pour it on me God, I can handle it." To the contrary, when things were good, being a man of extreme gratefulness, he would often burst out with a "God, I love it." These stories are just a few of my favorite memories of some of the people and events that I loved growing up in Oswego, New York.

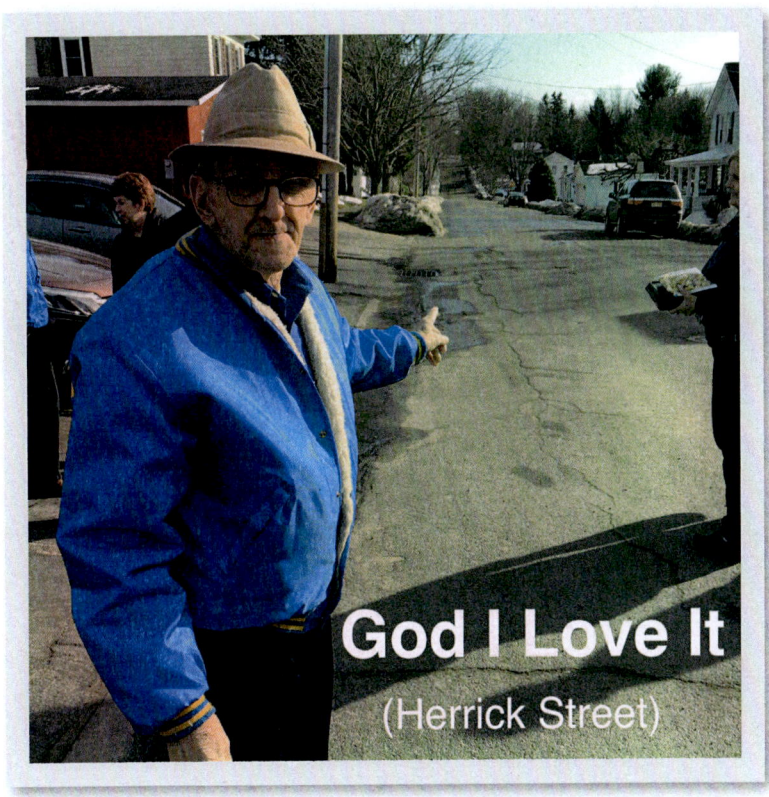

God I Love It
(Herrick Street)

Class of 71, the Fortunate One
Lucky, Grateful and Obligated

They say you can't judge a book by its cover, but in the case of the Oswego High School's Class of 1971, you can. Our Paradox was one of only a couple of yearbooks, over the many decades, that displayed unique artwork, which conveyed the exact sentiment of our class as well as a sign of the times.

The amazing cover of our yearbook was the art work of Margie Turner Fitzsimons. Margie was one of the approximate 350 students in the overcrowded old high school that stood near the corner of West First and Utica streets from 1921 to 1971. The school was so crowded it needed to go to "Split Sessions," Juniors and Seniors in the morning, and Freshman and Sophomores in the afternoon.

Yes, it was overcrowded, but the resilient class of '71 not only survived it, we thrived. Sure, just like every other class that graduated from our High School, we thought we were special, but there was a subtle sense that we were, indeed, just a little more extra special. With that feeling came the awareness that we ought to do something a little more too. I feel we did, as we felt a combination of lucky, grateful and obligated.

Lucky: We were lucky and we knew it. We were taught by some of the greatest teachers. There were seasoned teachers with many years of experience and fresh new ones with the energy and hearts of lions. Loschiavo, Familo, Kingston, Clyne, Simmons, Bartello, Zakur and Mantaro, were just a few of my favorites at the time. Talk about lucky, I was actually blessed to be taught history by the city historian, Mr. Anthony Slosek. He was brilliant and kind; we were his last batch of students.

Then there were those split sessions. Many of us loved them as they allowed us to sleep in for our first two years of high school and then work or play sports in the afternoons in our last two. Being a Trionfero, I chose to work full time (35 hours a week) at Vona Shoes just down the street through my whole upper-class time. My dad was so proud. Just as important, our school and its crazy schedule offered us electives to pursue hobbies and careers, and those split sessions gave us the time to work on those dreams!

Grateful: Looking back, we are so thankful that we were raised in the 1960s and 1970s in the wonderful city of Oswego. It had its many individual neighborhoods with multitudes of strong and decent families. We didn't appreciate it at the time, but we were so connected and we all felt safe. Because of this, we could play with our friends and neighbors and "hang out" till the street lights came on. A strong, lasting bond was created.

Obligated: With great gifts comes grate responsibility. We were (and are) so fortunate to have been the last class of that school. The building that was built in 1921, that housed our parents as students, made our community and the world a better place. You see, they weren't just our parents, we were BLESSED to be raised by "The Greatest Generation." Let us not forget, we were the last eyewitnesses to a generation that made the world better by teaching their kids to be kind, loving and peaceful. We were the next in a long line of succession who would be pressed to pass these admirable attributes onto our children and grandchildren.

Fifty years after Margie captured the sentiment of our class and times with that wonderful drawing, I stumbled upon my old yearbook one day. I had two powerful feelings.

First, we nailed it with that cover and we didn't even know it. Our yearbook cover conveys PATRIOTISM, PEACE AND LOVE. It is the absolute remedy for what's wrong for our country today. It must be all three together. Those three things are the formula needed to live in a peaceful city, country or world. The kind of UNITED world that we all want our children to grow up in. If we don't have all three together… we have nothing.

Second, the class of 1971's famous yearbook cover defined us and should inspired us to do good. It calls on us all to contribute to society as a good citizen just like our parents, the Greatest Generation, did before us.

Our class was the only class that was represented with that unique artwork symbolizing peace and love. Is it just a coincidence? Someone once told me that "a coincidence is just God's way of remaining anonymous."

We were taught proper and are called to pass the torch. Let us pass on the wisdom and love that our parents showed us to the generations to come. Let us prove we are, indeed, grateful and blessed.

Cover designed by:
Margie Turner Fitzsimons

'71

Oswego High School Class of 1971 Thanks The Greatest Generation

Bentley Warren and Oswego Speedway

A picture of my favorite childhood memories wouldn't be complete with a visit to Oswego Speedway. Back in the 1960s my first independent outings, in my teenage years, were to the "races." Officially it's called Oswego Speedway and sometimes it's referred to as the "Steel Palace."

I went often with my childhood friends, Alfie Castle and Stanley Falise. We lost Al Castle recently and while reminiscing about him, I showed a picture to my grandkids, hanging on my wall. It was of Bentley Warren my favorite driver at Oswego Speedway.

It was taken in the winner circle on August 26, 1967. As I was describing the "who and what" of this snap shot of my youth, I was reminded of how special the place, the people and that driver were to me. Here is why this picture is, as Bentley would say, is "Wicked cool."

1st. Bentley was my idol. I remember him first catching my eye driving the "speed kat" (black 01) in 1966. We always sat in the first turn so I could clearly see that front left tire coming off the track in turn two. I knew then he was courageous, talented and crazy. I loved him!

2nd. That August 26th night was so special. About four weeks earlier, Bentley flipped his car, "The Little Deuce," right in front of me during the warm ups in turn one. I was shattered and I thought his career was over. When, about a month later, he wins in the #21 car, everyone was shocked and delighted. (His arm was still injured from that wreck in July.)

3rd. I am in that picture holding another picture I had bought that night of his car flipping a month earlier. Also, in that picture you can see, "Alfie," his cousin Stanley, and my cousin Frank Maiurano. (who also passed away this year). There's a lot of people in that picture, but I couldn't help but notice the two young boys (in the front left) also looking at Bentley like he is God, waiting to get their programs signed.

Of course, I know that Nolan Swift built that place and Jimmy Shampine, who was taken way too soon, probably would have been the greatest ever. I am also aware that Eddie Bellinger, Jr. will always be the prince of the 5/8-mile track. I always cheered for "Eddie B" out of respect to the Oleyourryk family, as they were big fans and lifetime friends of the Trionfero Brothers.

But it's Bentley, whose picture is hanging on my wall. It's Bentley who, in his eighties, is still a legend to me. I have a photo on my desk, that my brother

Ken took in 2024, of our favorite driver sitting on the wheel of the restored "Little Deuce" in Watkins Glenn.

Oswego Speedway has millions of memories for so many of us "kids" from Oswego, New York. If I close my eyes, I can still smell the combined smell of popcorn and the exotic fuel. I can still see Clyde Rowlee waving that checkered flag for Bentley and I can still hear the great Pete Trenca yelling, "Programs!"

Harborfest, The View from the Stage

For its first thirty years, I had the privilege of being the emcee/entertainer for the Kid's Parade of the great Oswego Harborfest. I was granted this honor when I was approached by Mayor John Sullivan, and his lovely wife Charlotte, to be the first act ever for the inaugural "fest," in 1988.

It would be for the very first Thursday "kickoff event." In fact, the first Harborfest stage I performed on wasn't a stage at all. I set up on the cement steps of the old Post Office across from City Hall on West Oneida Street. It remained there for a few years before the opening ceremony was moved to Brietbeck Park. Those were my favorite years! My job was to entertain, organize, thank the sponsors and pass out lost kid tags.

Now, at 72 years old, I realize some of those kids I entertained, back in the early days, are in their '50s and '60s. Although I gave up the job a few years ago, (after my 30th year) I've been doing a lot of reminiscing lately and I found myself recalling my fondest memories of Harborfest. My view from the stage gave me a unique perspective of what it was really about. What I loved most about it; FAMILIES. My family, your Family and the Greater Oswego, NY family.

My Family: Harborfest was a Holiday in the Trionfero family. It was a multi-generational thing. We all showed up. My dad was there every single year with his Show of Love or JTS Music shirt. My brothers and sister were always in the audience. Nieces, nephews, cousins and aunts were often on the stage with me. Even my grandmother, Agnes Gorton, got to see me perform in those first few years as she lived just down the street at St. Luke's Apartments. She once sang, "For the Good Times."

My fondest memory of all, was bringing my grandkids with me year after year. I had 11 grandkids, so there were many fights for one of the coveted (5) seats available. We had to leave one open as we always picked up Great-Grampa on the way to Oswego. They sang, they danced and they laughed with their grampa and Great Grampa. This wonderful family tradition created so many precious memories.

Your Family: It was a city wide "Homecoming." Year after year I would witness the magical transformation of Oswego as its families reunited. Seeing entire families together again as I remembered them from my youth. Many times, I would "encourage" some of them to come up together to sing, dance or play. Many class reunions would be scheduled around Harborfest to take advantage of this vast migration home. Speaking of which, thanks to Marilyn Price Kovarik and the committee for all the years of work that they have done that allowed me to see so many of my fellow classmates from 1971.

The Oswego Family: My sister Rosanne said it best when she said "It's as though they put a giant tent over the whole city of Oswego and we have this ultimate family picnic." She was right. I think of all the groups that would come together. None better, for me, than when Jim Farfaglia would bring his Camp Hollis kids to the "party." I loved to see those buses. I will never forget the smiles on those kid's faces.

I would be remiss if I didn't thank Barb Manwaring for all those years of bringing me back. I appreciate her and the opportunity she provided me with. A little-known miracle of Harborfest is the kid's parade was NEVER rained out in all my 30 years. I am not sure if that was God or Barb.

In closing, the fireworks were magnificent, the music, as our Dad would say, was "Top shelf," the food great, but, …….. from my perspective, from the stage, it was always the Families coming together that truly made Harborfest great!

175

Oswego Baseball

Baseball has always been a huge part of Oswego's history and Fort Ontario was always the mecca that hosted thousands of baseball games. Those well-groomed diamonds supplied multitudes of young athletes with their own field of dreams and memories. Many of us players and spectators can remember a lot of those chilly evenings on the north shore of Lake Ontario.

So many teams have graced these fields with their presence. So many Oswego kids have played on both Little League and the Babe Ruth teams. One such team, that I happen to be very familiar with, was the Masons of the Babe Ruth League in the mid-1960s. That was my brother Marshall's team. My Dad and I went to all of their games.

It was my second favorite player who inspired this story. Joe Annorino was like the Micky Mantle of Oswego. He once hit a ball over the left field fence and the road behind it…. by a mile. He was Oswego, New York's own "natural." When Joe asked me if I had a team picture of the Masons, I was delighted to accommodate my childhood hero. Of course, my brother Marshall still had the team picture he had saved. (Joe would eventually switch interest, and become one of Oswego's greatest drummers.) I couldn't tell you all of the players' names now, but back then I knew who they were, their batting averages and what side of the plate they spit on when they stepped out of the box.

I also have vivid memories of the Harry Lagoe field. There were green bleachers, the same smell of grass and the mystical concession stand under the bleachers. I would tease my dad continuously for snacks. I remembered my brother's teammates families sitting and cheering in the stands.

What I remembered most were the smiles on everyone's faces watching the game. Baseball brought so much joy to all of the families back in those days. And to think, not one of the parents was on a darn cell phone. Coincidence.... I think not.

I would like to take a moment to thank all the moms and dads of Oswego Baseball history who rushed through (or skipped) many a meal to get their kids to the game on time. I remember our dad sometimes watching our games between working two long shifts at the papermill on Mitchell Street. Oh, how I smile when I think of Jenny Rinaldo cheering on her boys from the bleachers while occasionally chewing out the ump.

And did I mention those chilly nights at the ballpark that somehow warmed our hearts. Thanks for the memories, Oswego baseball and all of its players and spectators.

1968 OHS Basketball "Dream Team"
Chico Corradino Keven Riley Neil Miller Fred Borden Gary Cunningham

This legendary basketball team from OHS of 1968 was my "Dream Team" as a kid. I was playing for the St. Joe's team in the CYO league at the time and my older brother Marshall introduced me to yet another one of my most valuable childhood memories. I thought these players were better than the 1968 Knicks, but the truth is, I don't know how well they did in the standings, but they sure did win a lot of games.

What I do remember is Leighton Elementary School Gym was the hall of fame for young athletes like myself. It was an honor to get into those hallowed halls to watch our team play. What I remember most is these guys played as a team and were the epitome of good sportsmanship. They never were hot dogging (showing off). They just played the game right. They were icons to me. So tall and so talented. I absolutely loved those "boys."

My favorite player was Chico Corradino. He was my first experience with "cool." He was the "Fonzie" of Oswego, even before there was a "Fonzie." I remember how I wanted so badly to capture his confidence and coolness. I can picture

179

him, to this day, bringing the ball down the court with his chin up, his chest out and his left fist clenched. At 70, I still catch myself walking this way sometimes. I will never forget those hometown heroes.

VARSITY BASKETBALL

Left to Right: R. Polczak, G. Richardson, F. Borden, J. Pagano, G. Cunningham, N. Canale, Coach Dewey, N. Miller, J. Comini, J. Coniski, K. Riley, F. Michalski, F. Haynes

180

Oswego Jaycees

If you grew up enjoying the 4th of July festivities in Oswego, New York, it's important to remember where that extra specialness about the summer holiday, came from. It's a gift from the Oswego Jaycees that has roots going back over fifty years. I can't stress enough the positive impact that this wonderful civic organization had on our city.

I saw Bill Waters recently, a good friend and former Jaycee, and I was reminded of just how important these special men were to our city and myself. We should be especially grateful for their role in creating that first major summer holiday experience. It was usually the first Oswego holiday where we were sure it would not snow.

The Fourth of July celebration was full of energy and fun for the local families of the Port City. The parade was spectacular and became a big draw for some of the finest drum and bugle corps in the Northeast. The Mummers from Philadelphia were just one of the favorites. It was so much more than just a parade, since there was music, fireworks and a giant carnival with so many games and rides. It's thought by many to be the model and inspiration for Oswego Harborfest.

These Jaycees were just a bunch of local men that wanted to make a difference in their community, and boy did they ever! The 4th of July celebration was just the biggest event they had, but they did so much more. These guys were my friends, mentors and role models. In fact, it was my older brother Marshall who brought me in. I followed him where ever he went. (Music, working at Vona Shoes and the Jaycees)

The Jaycee's were eventually joined by the Jaynecees, and together these men and Women become pillars of the community. To this day, decades later, even the children of Oswego sense that our 4th of July celebration is just a little extra special. They just don't know why. Be sure to tell them about these men (and women) and their clubs.

Bill Waters, Mark Boutwell, Kevin Boutwell, Frank Klinger, Newell Chisell, Marshall Trionfero, Tom Price Joe Trionfero David Dice Dan Brown Chuck Durante and Jim Bushey.

"The Woodshed Tabernacle Choir"
(Featuring Bodie Schaffer)

I challenge anyone to find a nicer group of guys than those who were on the Woodshed softball team of the late 1970s. They were affectionately named, "The Woodshed Tabernacle Choir" by Paul Vandish and myself (Side by Side). They were kind, decent and fun-loving guys that were a great example of what this fine city of Oswego, New York, is built on.

I don't know all their names, but I do know Bodie Schaffer was one of the all-time greats, perhaps the "Duke of Earl" himself. (You had to be there.) Bodie was a gentleman, an athlete and the friend everyone would want. He was also the third unofficial member of our duo. He is pictured here performing his legendary version of "Let's Go to the Hop" at the Woodshed. I can still hear him singing his line; "Oh Baby." What a truly wonderful man he was.

It was his wedding night, when he and his beautiful bride Terry, showed up at the Woodshed, choosing to spend it with their friends. Thank you, Terry, for being a friend. Thanks to all those "Boys of Summer" for the great memories and their individual contributions to our city. You each made it just a little nicer.

(Thanks Robbie Corradino for encouraging me to write this, my first story, and providing me with the great photo that goes with it.)

"Top Self"
(Oswego Music Legends)

Although, not really a lesson, this was one of Dad's favorite phrases. Whenever something was particularly pleasing to our dad he would simply call it "Top shelf." Throughout my fifty years in the music business, dad was always my biggest supporters of every band I ever played in. "Top Shelf" was a title he would give each one of my bands (whether we deserved it or not). Being in the music business in Oswego my whole life, I thought it only fitting to include some of the many musicians that I felt truly deserved the designation of "Top Shelf." Over the last year I wrote several pieces entitled, "Oswego Music Legends." These are just seven of the greats that I thought deserved some extra attention. *(In alphabetical order, except for Paul Vandish.)*

185

Paul Vandish
"I'm at home at the piano"

A piano, a full set of drums and makeshift PA filled the room just off the living room in the Vandish home on 4th Street in Oswego, New York back in the 1960s. That little room was also filled with a big, beautiful sound. "It allowed me to pretend I was performing for the masses. It was quite loud and I'm not sure why our neighbors, the Roys, never openly complained. Every day after school, I was there." Who would have thought back then that, sixty years later, Paul Vandish would still be a young man belting out songs and filling large rooms with that amazing voice and his piano.

One thing's for sure, the Oswego native still fills a room with his incredible sound. What's his secret, how has he gone so strong for so long? Paul's fountain of youth is in his love for the music he plays, and the people he plays it for.

As for that full sound, Paul has a magic formula for that unique style that people gravitate to. Sure, he has an amazing voice, but the hidden ingredient is Paul was originally a drummer. It's this percussive style of playing combined with his unique left-hand bass that creates the original and full sound. It's always as though there's a couple of invisible members of his band.

Yes, Oswego's piano man, started out a drummer. First, he used pots and pans as a toddler, then with a plastic drum set he got one Christmas morning that was hidden in the family's laundry room. It all started at an age so far back Paul couldn't remember the beginning, but percussion seemed to stick for quite a while.

"What I do recall was that drums were my passion at that time. I remember in my early teens we formed a neighborhood band with Mark White (RIP) on guitar and Tom Price playing bass on a traditional six-string guitar and myself on drums and vocals."

Although his house always had an upright piano, Paul can only remember his sister playing it, as he had no real interest. While Paul did become an accomplished drummer, he had no idea that he was about to meet his real love, the piano. It was in his early teens when Paul finally found himself at the keys. "I'm not sure where the inspiration came from....my grandfather or my sister Karen."

Paul recalled visits to his grandparents' house where his grandfather would play songs for him like "Dark Town Strutters Ball," "Five Foot Two," and "Shine on Harvest Moon." "As time went on, somehow, I found myself playing chords and melodies and, of course, the songs that my grandfather had played for me. Although I couldn't, and still can't, read a note on a page, I could play that piano."

It was shortly after Paul graduated from high school when our mutual good friend, Tom Price, suggested that Paul and I would make a good musical team. He saw the magic before we did. This is when I met my lifelong friend and music collaborator. It was at this time that we both became members of the prestigious civic organization, The Oswego Jaycees.

Our first project was organizing a talent show at the old Oswego High School. Paul and I did a few songs and, although we did not compete, we rocked that auditorium. Paul Vandish and I started out what was to be a very successful endeavor that would last the better part of a decade side by side.

Paul's first real band was Patchwork. It was with the Barlow brothers, Bill and Jack, Phil Marshall and myself. This is when Paul had one of his major inspirations after seeing the Alligators at the Great Laker Inn. Paul held great admiration for this popular band and his dream was to join them and to play "The Laker." Paul stated, "I was no match to their keyboard player Rick Scapicchio (RIP). I met and talked with him once and he was a true gentleman and inspiration to me." Incidentally, it was The Alligators who inspired those famous white jumpsuits that Patchwork wore.

Paul and I briefly parted for a few months, as I wanted to do more "sophisticated rock." I soon returned to Paul, with hat in hand, to secure his amazing voice and, just as important, to return to the music Paul knew would make people dance and fill venues. The band Willow would become a brief hit covering Beach Boys, Beatles and the 1960s music. Paul was spot on and he taught me a lifelong lesson about playing to the crowd. Paul stated, "We had a great time traveling across the Northeast extensively with that band and eventually on our own Partridge Family bus. And I finally got to play at the Great Laker Inn!"

This is when the magic that Tom Price initially saw happened. Paul stated, "Our duo, Side by Side, was without question the highlight of my musical career. While Oswego was our hometown, a majority of our time was on the road full time, primarily playing to huge crowds at packed venues across the state." (Fifty weeks a year and 6 days a week.) We would draw hundreds out on a regular weekend night at the Auburn Holiday Inn. In fact, the Syracuse New Times (The main publication for music at the time) did a feature story on us.

It was at this stage in Paul's career that he connected the dots and truly realized what a blessing his parents were to him, "I must pay tribute to my parents for their support at that time, showing up and surprising me at the various venues we played across the state." Paul fondly remembered his parents letting him "set up shop" in that studio just off their living room.

When the end of Side by Side came, we saw the writing on the wall. Paul noted, "With culture changes like DWI enforcement and the arrival of HBO-style channels, people could choose other options for entertainment, and the music business would change permanently. There would be no more six night a week venue. It was not a great time to make a living with music." Paul and I both chose to go down other avenues and we both knew it was time to focus on our growing families.

Paul took an extended break from music. After the loss of his wife Kathy, who passed away after a long battle with cancer, he and his kids were just trying to find their way. Eventually, Paul found his way back by returning to his old friend music. In order to fill the void, Paul jumped back in with both feet and never looked back.

"I found my way back to sitting at the keys and singing to pass the time. I asked Gibby Thompson if I could play at his place and he graciously let me. Much to my surprise, my really good friends came out in droves to see me, and I had a new great solo career going." While Paul's initial thought was to play out once or twice a month, he was in huge demand by, of course, playing the music that people still wanted to hear…. and playing it well.

Paul's career would take another unexpected turn in his coincidental meeting with another Oswego Musical Legend, John Bletch. Paul offered, "One night, The Valch got rained out on the back porch of Gibby's with his band at the time and I was playing inside. He asked if he could set up his drums and play along. Does that surprise anybody?" Paul finished with, "It was a good chemistry, kind of like Oscar and Felix, one of us a rocker and me as a crooner. Double V's came from that and we have been together now for 15 years and are still going strong." Recently, I was delighted to hear that my lifelong friend had finally started to relax and take time for himself. Paul loves cruises.

Even there, the piano found him. Paul says, "Recently, I was on a cruise and frequented the piano bar. Ben, the entertainer, allowed me to sit in one night for a couple of songs and wow, did I have a blast! The crowd was amazing. I was at home behind that piano. Ben then had me up there every night after that. What an experience that was!" Paul wondered out loud, "I still wonder if I missed my calling, or whether it still might be in the cards. Cruising the world and getting paid for what I love doing!"

Sixty years later, Paul Vandish is still filling rooms, but now it's with sound and people. Over the decades, Paul has acquired a strong following of friends who pack the many top venues that he performs in. Paul holds a deep appreciation for his friends and always strives to give his audience 100%.

Back in the 1970s, Paul's duo guaranteed 20-minute breaks (with a timer) promising to buy a round for the house if they did not return in the allotted time. Today he takes little or no breaks. He once, at a follower's request, played for almost 24 hours straight, FOR FREE, for the Muscular Dystrophy Telethon. He might just be one of the hardest working guys in the business.

Paul is grateful to those friends he has made along the way. Without them he would have never had the life or career that he wished for as a kid when he pretended to play for the crowds.

"I never dreamed at this stage of my life that I would be playing out again and for sure not this much. I'm truly blessed." Paul's motto says it all, "Fun, Friends and Music, that's what it's all about." Paul is truly one of the all-time greats to ever come out of Oswego. My guess is the reason the Roys never complained about the sound from "The Kid" next door is because they, like everyone else, really liked the music.

Dan Batchelor
"Really, I'm Just a Time Keeper"

Question: Which Oswego Drummer, over the past 60 years, has drummed in a drum and bugle corp, a steel band in Barbados, on the streets of Toronto and, oh yeah, played with over **thirty local bands**, including some of the most iconic groups to every come out of our city?
Answer: Dan Batchelor

"Well, I've been around," was the response Dan said to me, with a chuckle, when I asked him if I could do one of my Music Legend Stories on him. I started to rattle off just a few of the bands that I knew Dan had been part of, before I could get through the first half dozen, he humbly piped in and said he was just a "fill-in guy." Believe me, Dan Batchelor was more than just a fill-in guy. When it came to percussion in Oswego, New York, he was "The Guy," and he is a legend.

This first occurred to me last winter, as I was compiling my Oswego Band List. Someone asked me if there were any musician's names that kept popping up on the list more than others. I checked and, yeah, there was one. "Batch," was a drummer who had played with dozens of groups, and on top of that extensive resume, he'd basically done it all.

194

Dan started drumming sixty years ago after being inspired by his idols in bands like The Valliants, Thunderbirds, and Billy and The Barons. His partner in crime, in the very beginning, was his good friend Norm Berlin. It was Norm who encouraged "DB" as a young teenager to play drums and to join him in a band to compete in the High School Junior Variety show. The crazy notion of two drummers in one band was just the tip of the iceberg when it came to Norm's vision and enthusiasm.

Dan actually first started out as a guitar player with a guitar he had purchase at nine years old from Fred's Record Shop on West Bridge Street. At eleven, he joined the Pathfinder Drum and Bugle Corp with his friend Norm. But it was after that talent show when Dan's career would first begin with the "US" Band, the band with the Fifteen Hundred Dollar Drum Sound. "My 1st band was really a result of our excitement over the British Invasion." The US band was launched after finishing second place in a battle of the bands at Three Rivers Inn. There, they would meet the popular "Dandy Dan" Leonard, of WNDR radio and their 1st real agent, Bill Andrews. As for those drums, Dan talks about his first set of Pink Champagne, Ludwig's, purchased in 1965, like someone else would talk about their favorite grandchild.

It was Dan's second band, T G and the Night Ryders, that hit pay dirt, as this local group stumbled upon an incredible chemistry that drew a cult-like following across the city. To this day, if you mention anything about this band, it stirs excitement that still simmers a half century later. Dan says, "We were playing the right music at the right time; Motown and R & B were popular and danceable." It was with the Night Ryders that Dan would begin his 50-year friendship and collaboration with fellow musician, the very talented Jim Schneider.

The next huge break that truly altered the course of his career, was when "Batch" met his good friend and lifelong mentor Eddie Goodness. He was introduced to Jazz and Swing. That sound, and those lessons from Eddie, stuck with Dan for the remainder of his career. "It was Eddie who taught me very early on you need to have big ears." Dan takes pride on learning that lesson, as he fondly recalls his friend, Jimmy Dillabough, a legendary Oswego bass player, telling Dan, "You are one of my favorite drummers because you really listen to me." Dan rounded out his versatile musical tool chest while playing the blues with Rockin' Ron and the Night Crew.

The Oswego native's natural talent was obvious to everyone, as Dan was often the first call made for that "fill-in guy," when a drummer was needed. With his abilities, Dan could have gone anywhere and everywhere but, luckily, found out early on that the road wasn't for him. "I'll never forget, I was asked to go on the road with Denise Week's Red Velvet band, back in the '70s. They had a gig in Rutland, Vermont, and after an extended engagement in the New England town, the band decided to swing by to their next gig in Muncie, Indiana." Dan laughed, "I told them there were a lot of places to play along the way, but we just headed directly to Indiana for our next extended job."

The road just wasn't for Dan and, luckily for Oswego and its music community, he planted roots in the Port City. He never regretted his choice of staying local, as he was able to pursue many other avenues. While maintaining a full work and play schedule, Dan managed to acquire three degrees, including his Master's in business. He wondered aloud how he did it. "One time, I remember I was selling real estate for my day job, selling cars at Deal Maker Ford on the weekend, while all the time, having a full set of drums in the back seat of my car."

"DB'S" style is what sets him apart from a lot of other drummers, as he chooses to play with finesse as opposed to power. If you asked him, he would use the term "Dynamic." Back in the '70s we had a term that described Dan perfectly. It was, "tasty." He eloquently mixes a variety of equipment and technique to achieve a diverse and original sound.

"Sometimes, I'll use a brush in one hand and a stick in another. You're painting a picture, you're trying to create colors. You can't paint a fine picture with a five-inch brush." As for volume, Batch says so many bands today play so loud. "If you start out at full volume, you have no where to go." The influence of the master, Mr. E. Goodness, shows up again and again in the words and actions of this Oswego drummer.

In the end, Dan is not just one of those rare local legends who's still working in the business at the top of his game. DB is a seasoned and experienced professional who has been around long enough to have learned from his idols of the 1960s and then pass it on to the generations to come. If any of those younger musicians, or anyone else, would like to catch this Oswego legend, Dan continues to perform regularly with his group, Sweet Soul Project. This trio includes his long-time friend Jim Schneider and his partner Susan Boysman.

Dan's wisdom I expected, but his modesty surprised me. As I was telling him how much I admired his numerous accomplishments, he merely responded with, "Really, I'm just a timekeeper." Well, as a timekeeper, he is truly like a human metronome, but he is also a "time-defier." When the 74-year-old Dan Batchelor is setting behind those drums, he still SOUNDS, FEELS and LOOKS great.

More important are his outlook and his sense of purpose. "With all the negatives in the world today, I feel music is my way of contributing a positive action towards spiritual happiness." Dan is a music legend in Oswego, New York, and our city was lucky to have had him for the last sixty years. Based on another Goodness-Batchelor quote, he'll be around a bit longer. "You don't want to show everything you got. You have to hold something back; you have to have somewhere to build." We all look forward to seeing "The time keeper's" next sweet project.

Faye Beckwith (and Anticipation)

In Oswego, New York in the 1970s if someone asked the question, "What band are you going to see tonight," the answer was probably Anticipation. If anyone asked where they were playing, the answer was, everywhere. For a period of about 15 years, if you were going into a bar, bowling alley or wedding reception, you would probably be greeted with the soft and familiar sounds of that band, the minute you walked through the door. Anticipation, with Faye and Jack Beckwith, was the city of Oswego's house band. They were "soft rock" before it became a thing. They were a hugely popular group that could make you get up and dance and yet still allowed you to have a conversation with the people you were "hangin" with.

Anticipation happened to me at a special time in my personal development in the music business. I was in my early twenties, and interested in making a career of it, and from the very first time I saw them, I stood ready to watch and learn. They were the pros and I knew I was watching magic unfold in front of me. They had an innate ability to connect with their audiences. I recall being at one of the many wedding receptions I attended at the Elks Club (I swear they played them all) when I happened to noticed dozens of people just standing and watching them like it was a rock concert. Again, this was at a wedding reception. They were talented for sure, but they had something beyond talent. Some called it chemistry; others called it the "it" factor, but whatever "it" was, it worked well.

There's no denying that the stage presence of a beautiful lady as a lead singer helped, but Faye Beckwith was much more than just a pretty face. Her softspoken style and grace at centerstage was classy and professional. And, oh yeah, that girl could sing! What I don't think a lot of people realize was she was not just a great singer, she was the first, solid female member of any band in our Port City. The music business in Oswego was a profession that had been mostly dominated by the "the boys in the band." Faye blasted through barriers and stereotypes to become the first Lady of rock and roll in our hometown. Faye stated, "In the beginning, I was just an observer with three babies." She wanted more, she could do more. Turns out, she didn't just do more, she did it all. Faye Beckwith was always a force to be reckoned with.

If that weren't enough, she happened to be standing on stage, side by side with her husband Jack, and that made it all the more special. He wasn't just her husband; Jack was the love of her life. That chemistry was obvious. It was like that bond we all noticed between Sony & Cher or Springsteen and his wife Patty. You knew your witnessing something a little extra special on that stage.

Speaking of Jack Beckwith, we all know he was the leader of the band, but there was something else that made that band a huge success and that was Jack's tremendous business acumen. He was a natural born salesman. He was the promoter before they were even called that. He got the bookings and somehow everyone in the city magically knew where Anticipation was playing. That was no fluke. Jack's band ran like a well-oiled machine and, although money was never their goal, Anticipation created a very lucrative business model. Even as a young man I noticed the master at work, I did take notes and they helped me throughout my entire career. Thank you, Jack.

Of course, Faye and Jack did not do it alone, but, in yet another way, they succeeded since they always surrounded themselves with very talented people. Jimmy Holmes, Burt Phillips, Tom Green and Billy Skipper, just to mention a few.

Anticipation was a band that made history in Oswego NY in the 1970s. The group was extraordinary in so many ways. Let it be known to all you young female performers out there, when you are commanding the stage at you next venue, it's Faye Beckwith that you have to thank. She was the trailblazer who first opened that door. When I asked Faye if she encountered a lot of difficulty with those barriers, stereotypes and limitations that so many women faced back then her response was "I didn't see them, I wouldn't see them." That says it all about this formidable woman.

Jack and Faye have been partners now for over sixty years at home and over fifty years on stage. I asked Faye if we might still see the happily married couple out on stage when she quipped, "You still might see us gigging out there somewhere."

It was on March 17th, 1972, that Anticipation was transformed into action as that band did their very first show. Since then, thousands of people have witnessed the magic that Faye and Jack conjured up on that stage. Truth be told, I was one of those dozens of people that stood and watch those "rock stars" at that wedding reception. I remember thinking, how cool is that. I want to do that someday.

Jack and Faye, your band is a legend. You didn't just make money. As your newer band card says, you made music, memories and fun for us all. You didn't just entertain thousands of people, you inspired some of us too. Thank You for sharing your song. (A beautiful duet.)

Burt Phillips,Jim Holmes,Dave Parkhurst, Jack & Faye Beckwith, Tim Green

Anticipation

204

The Loschiavo Family

"Our Dad's love of music, to me, was displayed in the way he would take his saxophone out of its case. He had this case with a purple velvet liner. When he opened it, it was like a treasure chest, you could tell music was his treasure."
Joe Loschiavo

Loschiavo, was a name you knew if you followed good music during the '60s and '70s in Oswego NY. Whether you performed with, or were spellbound by, one of these talented Loschiavo "kids," you knew who they were.

Joe, Chuck, Christine and Tom were household names in our city, as the four gifted musicians from just one family seemed to shine everywhere. Their dad, Charles, was the accomplished musician who planted those seeds that would leave their permanent mark on the Oswego music scene.

Noah and the Arkmen, Octavius, Steppan, Arena, The Manic Depression, The New Brotherhood and The Leo Bloom Group were all popular bands who earned their loyal followers and stellar reputations. The Loschiavo siblings that graced those bands were not just masters of their craft at a young age, they were schooled musicians who a had knack for surrounding themselves with the very best talent that Oswego had to offer.

They were also trailblazers in the industry introducing one of the first female singers in a rock band, the first horn band doing Chicago and Santana tunes, and the first group to offer the incredible (and heavy) sound of a full Hammond Organ with a Leslie Speaker setup as well. Their music was always top quality.

Joe is now an accomplished keyboard player who's never left his lifelong friend, music. The oldest brother is a solo pianist who still loves performing at various venues, including private parties, receptions and special events. Joe is a gifted composer who, while performing at the Greenbrier resort in White Sulphur Springs, West Virginia, composed the very beautiful "Allegheny Waltz." Joe has written many other songs and has produced four CD's. His entire catalog is available on all the major music platforms. His latest, "What Have You Done" is sung by Oswego's own Cam Caruso. (can be found on YouTube)

Chuck Loschiavo was always a great lead guitarist and vocalist. I remember my good friend John Readling always telling me about this incredible Chuck Loschiavo. They had shared time in the super group, Octavius. It was Chuck's love and involvement with bands that propelled him into his lifelong career. "I moved down to the Philadelphia area right after graduation from RIT to take a job. I was inspired to pursue electrical engineering because of my interest in rock band gear." He continued, "I did have a side music career for years in the Philly area, playing for a Neil Diamond tribute band and other classic rock bands." Anyone talking to Chuck could tell that, even though he followed other career paths, his love of music was always at his very core. It's still in his blood.

Christine Loschiavo Puzauskas, like her dad, loved to sing. She sang in the Oswego High School choir called the Philomelians for four years. In her first year at SUNY Oswego, Chuck invited her to sing in Manic Depression and the Arena. The brothers were admittedly shocked when Chris first showed them her amazing ability to change her image dramatically. The lead singer's siblings fondly recalled how their talented sister could nail Gracie Slick's "Somebody to Love", like she did for the packed house at the Oswego Theater for the DG Premier.

Chris was one of the very few female singers in Oswego and she was one of the overall best! Being a Loschiavo, she, of course, transformed her love of singing and music into her creation of a nonprofit. Flight 33 Inc. supports youth with their education by sponsoring an afterschool program in Guadalupe, Arizona. Students are also given the opportunity to expand their horizons by taking music lessons and doing art projects.

Tom would forge his own path following his famous father's footsteps starting in school, playing trumpet for jazz band, Marching Band, Symphonic Band and Wind Ensemble. In high school, he played under the direction of Ed Lisk and he started with the trumpet with Lenoard Lambert as his teacher.He also played lead trumpet for three years with the renowned Oswego State Solid State band under the direction of Hugh Burritt and Jerry Exline. The younger Loschiavo told of the pride he felt, at 13 years old, performing with his dad in the Oswego City Band. He was just as proud to have been one of the youngest card-carrying members of the local musician's union. Tom continues to play, taking up the drums at age fifty.

The well-known dad, Charles Loschiavo, was the one who blasted the pathway open for his talented brood. The family Patriarch played Sax and Clarinet in the Oswego City Band, beginning when he was 15 years old. He performed with the Army Air Corp Band for four years and then came home to continue with the Oswego City Band for a total of 70 years. He played his entire music career with the Nick Stereo Orchestra, in which band members became like family. He sat and played side by side with is friend Mr. Stereo for decades. The kids would fondly recall how their dad would often return home from his shows with cupcakes, cookies or cake wrapped up in napkins.

Charles loved to sing, if not in the orchestra, then with St Joe's choir or just belting out "Ol Man River" into a tape recorder he borrowed from school. That amazing baritone voice also served him well for over twenty years as he was also the announcer for that iconic Oswego City Band. The seasoned professional would often sit in for his children's rock bands for many wedding receptions and more sophisticated events when his kids' sound needed to be classed up a bit.

Let there be no mistake, it was their dad, Charles Loschiavo, who was the common denominator and the hidden ingredient in all the kid's love for, and success in, the music business.

The wide success of this talented family went far beyond musical genetics, as the father's support and encouragement, for his own fab four, was enthusiastic and unconditional. He always went above and beyond. Chuck stated, "I'm still amazed he let me play my first college fraternity party when I was only 13 years old and only in the eighth grade. So many times, he would come and pick us up at one or two in the morning." Tom also credits his dad as being his biggest inspiration. Chuck added, "I think our work ethic was definitely a reflection of our parents. Our dad was especially supportive of our rock careers even though he was solidly in the Jazz and American Songbook traditions."

Fast-forward fifty years and so much has changed. The one constant that has remained is the love of music that their dad instilled into all of them. Nothing speaks to this more that the fact that they still reunite for a reunion gig every year or so to play, sing and laugh with family members and friends. They still love playing the classic rock songs they once played as kids. Brother Chuck jokes, "It was just called rock back in those days."

The Loschiavo story would not be complete without the mention of the other artists of the family. The matriarch, Mary Loschiavo, and the youngest child Margaret (Meg). Although not musicians, they were also outstanding in their fields.

"Mrs. Losch" was a gifted art teacher and painter. Her incredible creativity and infectious smile inspired so many students. It also gave a whole other perspective of the arts to her own five children. The loving mother also enjoyed working on theater projects at Oswego State with set designs. She often had her own kids help with her many art shows and seemed to always have her students' posters laid out around the house.

Meg took after her amazing Dad. The youngest of the five children, followed in "Mr Losch's" English, journalism, and writing skills. She has recently completed her first novel.

Meg's website says: *"Margaret Goss is a creative writer, devoted mom, and registered nurse. Her early appreciation for the arts was inspired by her parents – first-generation Italian-Americans. Her debut novel, "The Uncommitted," began as a tribute to her father, an English and Journalism teacher, as well as musician, and her mother, a gifted art teacher and painter. Her second novel, a sequel to her first, is nearly complete."*

Meg is also a registered nurse who holds a Bachelor of Science from Arizona State and a Master of Public Affairs and Administration from the University of Wisconsin-Madison.

The bottom line is anyone from Oswego's golden age would be hard-pressed to describe the Loschiavo family, or any of its members, in one word. As gifted as they all were, I am guessing the word would not be talented. Words like, joy, humility and goodness come to mind. They are the family's real signature. This is never more evident than when it was shown in that famous Loschiavo smile. That same smile that was created on the day that Charles and Mary tied the knot, back in 1950.

You see, what made the Loschiavos so special wasn't their ability to perform or create the art, it was their love of the art itself, and sharing it with others. Their love of family and friends was always

211

bigger than the song, painting or book. Sure, they're all outstanding artists, but, more important, they are all upstanding people and good citizens. This is what their lovely parents would be so proud of.

Oldest brother Joe tells one final story that says it all and places a bow on this beautiful family package.

"My brother Tom arranged for a local sound engineer to record my father on sax. He was 87 and residing in a memory care unit in Chandler, Arizona. Despite all this, he could still play well." After the patriarchs passing at 91, Joe added keyboard tracks to his father's songs. The father & son's version of Ruth Lowe's, "I'll Never Smile Again," is as magical as it is heartfelt. This song is symbolic, as it shows the very special bond this family shares will never be broken. Not even by time or distance.

The legendary dad, Charles Loschiavo, will have a legacy that will live on in the music, memories and actions of his five kids and their families. The symmetry is perfect. On Father's Day, 2025 the dad that started it all got one more ovation in his kids hearts and minds. They will all honor and remember him every time they open their own treasure chest.

Standing: Tom Chris Chuck Joe

Charles & Mary with baby Meg

The Loschiavo's

Chris Joe Chuck Tom Meg

213

John Luber

If you're from Oswego, New York, then sometime during the last fifty years you have probably heard the name Johnny Luber. If you happen to be a musician, then I am pretty sure you not only know the name, but you've most likely heard his amazing guitar speak to you. If you are actually one of the lucky musicians who has played in one of John's 50 bands, in over the last half of century, then count yourself lucky to have played with one of the all-time greats. Johnny Luber is a legend, a rare icon who happens to remember every band he's ever played in and every person he's ever shared a stage with. Each and every one is important to him.

His very first guitar would come in 1964 as a Christmas gift from his parents which they bought from Montgomery Ward. John says, with a chuckle, "It was a Kingston guitar that came with an amp that had only a volume control and no tone controls at all." John also spoke proudly of wanting that guitar badly as he was inspired by his Uncle Jack Connolly, (of the Valiants), another Oswego music legend. John would briefly take guitar lessons from Mrs. Hart, but soon found he was way ahead of the class as he was playing chords before the others were learning the notes.

Perhaps it was an omen when, in the summer of 1968, Father Buckel, of St Mary's Church, offered

John's first band, called Midnight Streak, to play in the church basement (Hopkins Hall) for $15.00, and then paid the band $25.00 instead. It would be the first of many times that John's real talent and value would quickly become apparent to anyone who heard or seen him play.

John's second band, Age of Innocence, taught him a valuable lesson as he recalls being the warm up band for "We the People," a band a bit out of his league. This started him on a very long journey of always wanting to get better. After a short break and selling his guitar, Luber came back with a new $80.00 guitar that he saved up for by working odd jobs. The first band was appropriately called Birth, as it was the beginning of a very long and successful career. The Oswego native never looked back nor slowed down again.

A band that inspired him in the early 1970s was Bill Carnal's Panacea. As for John, Shadow Fax, Backtracks, The Funky "Dairnt" Band and Fission were just a few of his early bands during that 1st full decade of playing out. When I asked John what his favorite band was, he eloquently said, "Regardless of the band or music they played, I respected them all, as long as it was done right."

When I asked what his favorite type of music was, he responded that he liked a rhythmic style of

215

guitar and lead. He was proud of his own special style. "I'd hope that when someone walked into a bar and heard the band playing they could tell it was me before looking up to the stage." David Quigley, Paul Jude Heagerty, Tom McGrath, David Burritt and Jerry Renino were some of the people that he really clicked with who offered him a rhythm section that allowed his lead guitar to shine.

Luber would be one of the few Oswego musicians to delve into bar ownership after buying the Shacki Patch, a local favorite, known for its great bands and music. John not only showcased his bands, such as the Melons and Mr. Cucumber, but also brought in some great out of town bands like the Kingsnakes of Syracuse.

Johnny Lubers talent and career would not be limited to the Shacki Patch or even Oswego as he quickly garnished statewide fame thanks to his extraordinary talent and a little help from a Syracuse agent at DMR. The Critics was just one of his bands known and admired throughout New York. He was even invited, at one time, to New York City by an A&R executive from Atlantic Records. Another great memory of John's was playing the Syracuse Blues Fest with his band "2 kool 4 Skool." Speaking of great band names, always a great promoter, the clever Luber also came up with perhaps the best band name ever, calling his crew the Luber Cators.

In the music business they say you can tell greatness by the number of great people you have played with, and John is the epitome of that. Of course, he has played with many of the great local musicians but he has also crossed paths with some real pros on the national scene. Yes, Vanilla Fudge, Carmen Appice and the Monkees are just a few that John has brushed elbows with. John has actually shared the stage with Peter Tork and Micky Dolenz, of the Monkees; David Johnson from the Nevills; Geo, the bass player from Gloria Estefan's band; and Lee Thornberg, the legendary horn player from Chicago and Tower of Power. Luber has also warmed up for legendary bands such as Steppenwolf, 4 Tops, Wilson Pickett and 3 Dog Night. However, this time he was not nervous as he was up for the challenge.

For the past 12 years, venues up and down the West Coast of Florida, from Tampa to Marco Island, have enjoyed and been duly impressed with Oswego's own Johnny Luber. The hometown hero talks fondly of all the great southern musicians he has worked with, as well as the recently passed performer Hurricane Harvey. The fact he remembers, and reveres, every band and musician he has ever played with speaks volumes about John's love of the business and his respect for his bandmates. Despite his incredible talent, he was always a team player.

A couple of people that he remembers fondly were Barry James McCaffrey, another guitar legend; and close friend Billy Feeney. John said "Barry was an incredible writer and a great guitar player and they always pushed each other to become better players." Of his friend Bill Feeney, "Billy was a true friend since childhood. We played together as kids and then we played together as bandmates." Both McCaffrey and Feeney would be lost at a very young age.

In his 70s John continues to perform his unique style of guitar as a solo artist and with anyone that needs or wants his expertise. John is kind of proud of the fact that he had become "A gun for hire" in the business. He also continues to practice, as he still strives to become better. His reputation is stellar and he is always in demand by venues and bands alike. Since that first night in Hopkins Hall, 57 years ago, in St Mary's Church basement, so many bands have wanted this local icon at the center of their stage.

So many of us, from Oswego sees this "kid's" talent and understand his value. John, we are proud to call you our own and you are a legend. Thank You for sharing your gift with your Port City family.

John Luber

MICHAEL

You know you've made it to the top in the music business when all you need is your first name to be recognized. MICHAEL, of Oswego, New York, is one of the few who earned that honor starting back in the 1970s and still maintains it to this day. His career spanned six decades, and he accumulated the most remarkable following I have ever seen in my hometown. He has assembled a fan base that he truly deserves because he is a great entertainer who has always respected and appreciated the friends he has made along the way. Michael Pauldine, although truly a humble man, deserves the accolades and admiration shown to him over his 60 years of performing. He's is a good guitar player, an excellent vocalist and most important, a charismatic showman.

What's kind of funny is that a performer, with such a successful music career, fought off music as it tried to chase him down as a kid. While his music teacher, Miss Scriber, and others recognized his musical potential, Michael just wanted to play baseball. Eventually, it caught up to him and he could no longer hide his talent as Gary Stevens and Walt Koken convinced Michael into joining his first band, the Kings 3. It was in this group that he would meet his friend Sam Domicola. Although Michael was a bit reluctant to pursue his musical career initially, in February of 1964 that all changed, as he would get hooked upon hearing his first Beatle record. At the time, being in more of an acoustic act, Michael remembers his exact words saying, "We're going to need a drummer."

The Newberry 4, the band founded by Michael, was huge in the 1960s in Oswego, as they were literally everywhere. They also achieved a great level of recognition when releasing their popular hit record, "I Think I'd Love You," a great song which received significant airplay in the Syracuse market as well. The Newberry 4 would also be one of the first bands I would see as a kid. I was deeply influenced by its rock star singer. Did I mention the girls loved Michael too, as he not only could sing and play like a Beatle, but he also looked like John Lennon.

His bands at that time included, at one time or another: Chip Riley, Tom DeSantis, Tony Marturano, Skeets Murabito, Sam Domicolo and George Smith. Tom, George and Skeets would be three connections that Michael would maintain and treasure from then on. In fact, it was George's late wife Rosie who, unknowingly, launched MICHAEL into the stratosphere of Oswego Music. After watching the Newberry 4 perform one night, Rosie told him. "The best song you do is Thank the Lord for the Night Time, by Neil Diamond. The seed was planted. Michael also formed the band Promise that included myself, Skeets, George and the late Buddy Murray (who was an awesome guitar player and a great man). After a brief stint as a duo with Sam Domicolo in 1975, MICHAEL became the first single act in Oswego.

Michael was solid from day one, as he started his "solo career" long before technology offered assistance, such as MIDI sequencing. His golden voice and incredible stage presence commanded his audiences as he would pack the local venues and he could make those cash registers sing too. The term pop star comes to mind as Michael was so popular that fans and friends would travel from far and wide to catch his performance. This aspect also drew him out of Oswego as the "MICHAEL" brand became a huge success in the greater Syracuse and Rochester Markets. He had many opportunities presented to him to go as far as he wanted, but chose to stay close to his family and friends in Central New York over national success.

Michael was not only just the first solo act in Central and Western New York; he was a trailblazer in one other big way. He, in fact, was the first ever "tribute band," as he was paying homage to Neil Diamond, as far back as the 1970s. He covered Diamond's voice and sound with an uncanny precision. It was always his intention to just merely fulfill the request of his enthusiastic audience who

continually requested, "More Neil Diamond."
Michael stated, "I identified with him as a singer,
songwriter and as a decent person who always kept
his stardom in check." This aspect of Pauldine's
career propelled him to a level of popularity
and success rarely achieved by many other CNY
performers.

Despite his incredible success he never let it go
to his head. When I asked Michael who or what he
attributed his success too, the only thing he humbly
mentioned was his parents who, through their
wisdom and love, supported him into his lifelong
career. Sure, he could cover Neil Diamond, and that
performer from Oswego could pack them in, but,
after sitting with my friend Michael for a few hours,
I uncovered the real reason this man's career was
as hot, as a "Hot August Night." It was his love and
loyalty to the music and his many followers.

The absolute proof of this was in his massive
photos collection. When I asked this icon for a
simple promo picture to use for this story, Michael
was hard pressed to find one. In fact, we went
through thousands of pictures looking for that
picture of the "Star." Instead, what I saw was photo
after photo of Michael posing with one of his
multitudes of fans and friends. What stood out to me
the most was that the smiles and friendships were
real and the love and appreciation was mutual. Yes,

223

a star was born on Mohawk Street in Oswego New York, and MICHAEL's light still shines bright today. He is one star who will never fade.

George Smith
"I was Just a Lucky Guitar Player"

A guitar neck was sticking out of a garbage barrel sitting on Duer Street in Oswego, New York in the 1950s. An eleven-year-old boy, George Smith, took that guitar and made a lifelong friend. "Nobody wanted that guitar, which only had five strings, so I took it home and I played the heck out of that thing."

Over the next fifty years, George Smith would be playing the heck out of a few guitars. It all started around 1960, when the 12-year-old joined his first band, the Medallions. That band lasted a couple of years. George stated, "We were okay, but we were just having fun horsing around and making some noise." At 14, he and his good friend, Billy Musacchio, started a band that lasted a couple of more years. Although those bands never went too far, they allowed the Oswego native to save enough money to buy what would become, his favorite guitar. It was a Guild Starfire One. Shortly afterwards, he would be asked to join the Newberry 4 which launched his career into one of Oswego's premier bands of the 1960s.

In a time when most bands lasted only months, the Newberry 4 had the talent and chemistry to propel it forward for over a decade. George remembers being booked out months in advance. He recalled one of his fondest memories as a teenager. "We were at the YMCA Association Island camp for a whole week. At first, we were worried, as when we played no one was dancing. But they brought out chairs for the kids to sit in and we realized they were watching us like it was a rock concert."

Smith and his bandmates, Michael Pauldine, Chip Riley and Tony Marturano played hundreds of shows all over Central New York. George talked of a couple of his prouder moments. One was performing with the Ink Spots at Three Rivers Inn. A second was getting to jam with the guitar player from Tommy James and the Shondells as they shared the billing at the College Inn, a giant venue near Lake George.

One time, after renting their band's equipment out to Frankie Valli and the Four Seasons for a show at the Oswego State College, George said, "The Four Seasons got stuck in Ohio and called us to see if we would open for them and play until they arrived. When they finally got there, they watched us from backstage." He recalls, "As I was leaving the stage, Frankie Valli grabbed my hand and said, Hey kid, you're pretty good." The modest Smith chuckled, telling me, "Our band actually got paid twice, once for renting the equipment and then for being the opening act." These were just a few of the highlights that he could remember during his long and successful run. "It was a great band with really good singers and harmonies," George stated, as he spoke proudly of how Michael Pauldine once told him "When you joined the group, we got the music."

Smith's second band was called Promise. This was a band that had two configurations which lasted over three years. The first band had a tremendous horn section. The later included Buddy Murray, Sam Domicolo, Michael Pauldine, Skeets Muribito and myself. George enjoyed both bands but marveled at how good that horn band was.

Yes, I had the pleasure of playing in my first band with George, as he took me under his wing and showed me the ropes. I could not have asked for a better mentor as he was a kind and patient man. At the time, I was too young to realize that I was working with a unicorn. Here was a talented, popular musician who was also modest and down to earth. This soft-spoken man was one in a million. I couldn't believe he was my friend. The Oswego guitarist spent the remainder of his career with a couple of great local bands he enjoyed very much: Revival and Yesterday's Image.

Smith also had an incredible work ethic and it should be noted that throughout his entire career the father of four worked full-time jobs with Flexo Wire and almost twenty years, with The Miller Brewing Company. George recalled always working twelve-hour shifts at the brewing company while still performing six nights a week. He wasn't bragging; it was just a matter of fact.

George's personal life wasn't easy, by any measure. He lost his wife Rosie, after only 16 years of marriage. During my time in the band, I got to know Rosie, and oh, what a special and spirited lady. She was a kind soul who was just as beautiful on the inside as she was on the outside. Their daughter Kelly fondly recalls hearing that her mom often said, "I'm not here for a long time, I am here for a good time." George confirmed this when he mentioned his wife and mother of their four little girls, "Rosie was my partner, she was always along for the ride."

His childhood wasn't easy as well. He never knew his dad and ended up being raised by his grandparents, who he affectionally referred to as his best friends. Kelly says, "Music was always my dad's savior. It had a calming effect on his mental health." Anyone who had ever seen him play knew this by that coy smile on his face and the way he would close his eyes when he played. Music was always his escape.

When I asked George what was one of his greatest accomplishments he said, without hesitation, "Working with my idol, Buddy Murray." He told the story, "My older sister wanted to go to a high school dance, but she wasn't allowed to go unless she took her little brother. She finally relented and brought me with her," he said with a laugh. "She didn't have to worry about me hanging around her as I spent the entire night standing in front of the band watching Buddy Murray play. He was my inspiration." Smith got to play with his idol, a dream come true.

This legendary guitar player can no longer play, as arthritis has taken his hands. It would be a surprise to no one that his final contribution to the business he loved so much would be teaching several kids how to play guitar, including a few of his own grandkids.

He proudly proclaimed how his grandson downloaded a Newberry 4 song on his phone and played it for his music teacher. He said, "Poppy, my teacher thought it was the Beatles." The grandson was so proud of his Poppy, and truth be told, Poppy was pretty proud as well.

George would only allow that pride for an instant. When I mentioned his kids and grandkids should be proud of him and he was a star, the mild-mannered man came back with the perfect George Smith quote:

"I don't believe in the term star …. rock star, movie star or sports star. I believe if anyone gets to do what they really love, and make a decent living at it, then they should consider themselves lucky. I was just a lucky guitar player."

How lucky for us that the eleven-year-old boy on Duer Street spotted that guitar in that garbage barrel. George Smith may not realize it, but he is a legend in his home town of Oswego, NY.

Although he always wanted to stay out of the spotlight and fly under the radar, he couldn't help but shine. In a business full of big heads and egos this gentle-man was humble. He was also cool without even trying. He was a simple man who loved his family, his guitar and his music. George Smith never bragged, ever. He didn't need to. He let his guitar do the talking.

George Smith

"Don't Get Old"
(Old Age is Creeping in)

Being the eternal optimist he was our dad would always say, without a hint of sarcasm, "Old age is creeping in." He said this well into his 80s. He meant it. He also warned us thousands of times; "Don't get old." These stories are perspectives I have developed on aging from listening to my dad and watching him age with so much strength and grace.

"Old age is creepin' in
(Don't get old)

I'm Not Old, Yet

Recently, I was leaving my local hardware store with a 20 lb bag of bird food, when the nice young clerk named Zach approached me and said it. He took a quick glance at me and said those words that cut me like a knife: "Would you like me to carry that out for you, sir." The very sweet, well-intended young man was kind and thoughtful, but he might of just as well have picked up the nearby driveway stake, in aisle two, and stab me through the heart. Despite our smiles, it stung. I'm not old, yet!

I'm not quite sure if it was the grey hair, the laugh lines or the slight limp I mysteriously acquired while doing yard work that day. It didn't matter. He saw it and then he said it. I left that store, following the young man. He did carry that bag over his shoulder like it was a bath towel. On my way out, I purposely glanced at my reflection in the glass door to see what Zach saw. Oh my God, for a moment, I saw it too. The grey hair, the lines on my face. I swear It was my dad in that reflection. I could see it all and it was like a bee sting to my soul.

As I closed my car door and waved goodbye to the youngster, I pondered what had just happened. I soon stumbled down that preverbal rabbit hole of self-reflection. How could this nice young man not see the youth and energy I still possessed? Did he not know who I was? Couldn't he understand what I've done in my 71 years? Could he not imagine the work, play, sadness and joy that I had experienced during my time? Just for a second, I thought, could I be getting old?

It's hard to explain, but despite my myriad of ailments, I still feel strong and capable. I'm still alive. I still have the heart of a lion and make plans as though I'm a young man. However, I do also possess the knees and shoulders of a guy my age, not to mention a refrigerator door that's covered with magnets and medical appointments.

But wait, I'm still that young man that jumped, with my guitar, off a stage back in the 1970s. (Thus, the bad knees.) I am also the young ballplayer who broke up Gigsy Enwright's perfect game, with a base hit over second base, in 1966. I'm still the young stud that, in eighth grade, held a girl's hand and walked the entire two miles to Grant's Department Store. I want people to know THAT me, I want them to see THAT person.

I am not an old man. I'm still me. The one who has experienced my WHOLE life. I see, instead, a composite of the guy who has had an incredible seven-decade journey. Somehow, I have the ability to see everything I have done in an amazing collage of wonderful moments. Most importantly, I see it all in no particular order. Thank God, my life's memories and experiences are not just remembered chronologically. They are random, surprising and sometimes chaotic. I do remember. I was there. No, I am not an old man. I am a collection of memories and milestones that are painted vividly in every corner of my mind.

Truth be told, I've never really been insulted, outright, about my age. I do get reminded by family, friends and strangers about my "old age" as it gets implied or assumed. I do realize the "concern" is also a sign of love and respect. Of course, I understand that we all get old sooner or later, but I just soon it be later and at a time I decide.

I picture myself like Samson in that movie where he is pushing against those pillars of the temple. But for me, I see myself, arms outstretched, holding off old age as it's trying to crush in on me from both sides.

If you really think about it, that "Einstein thing," is profound. His theory of relativity says that time and space are only relative to the observer's frame of reference.

Let's say, for the sake of argument, that eternity is 953 trillion years long. I'm 71 years old and the young clerk is 21. That 50-year difference between us, compared to 953 trillion years, becomes completely insignificant. Thus, in regards to eternity, one precious moment and a whole lifetime, ultimately, have about the same value in time. In my remaining time, I am sure I still have thousands of those precious moments left, any one of them, potentially, having the same value as my entire lifetime. It's profound and it's all relative.

Despite the fact that I appear to understand all this, there are still times that I slip and fall, in my mind and on the front steps. I do forget things occasionally, thus sometimes I relent to the thought of aging. When I do start to think old, it's my wonderful wife Denise, not Einstein, who kicks my butt and reminds me, "Don't Let the Old Man In." (Toby Keith) What a powerful message. So simple. As usual, she's right.

I do have to go to the hardware store again soon. We need salt for our water softener. Those are actually forty-pound bags. I think I will let that nice young man carry it out for me. But, on the short walk to the car, we might just have a teachable moment. You see, I am going to tell Zach, and anyone else who will listen,

It's not just the "me" that I WANT you to see.
It's a whole life I've lived, that I WISH you could see.

Dedicated to the "Herrick St. Trionfero Family"

235

Aging Gracefully
(She said: "I'm the cat")

While performing at senior homes over the past 20 years, I have met many elders who have taught me a lot of lessons. "Never drive faster than my angels could fly." "Never do that which, if everyone did, would ruin society." "If horses were wishes, beggars would be riders." But, of all the lessons I've learned, the most important one was from a wonderful lady I met in Utica, New York at the St Luke's (Faxton) senior home.

Her name was Frances and she was first brought to my attention by the activity director of the facility before my show started. Tom Thorngren tugged at my elbow, pulled me aside and pointed Frances out. He said, "You see that lady over there, she's new here and is having a difficult time adjusting. She's a bit sad. Could you help her out?"

Tom had seen me work before and was requesting I do my magic and make that lady smile and possibly warm her heart. Frances, like so many others seniors I have met, had been recently "forced" to give up her home of many years. Many seniors are compelled to just walk away from the life they have lived and loved for so many decades. To make matters worse, more often than not, it's right after the recent passing of their lifelong partner. When I put myself in their

237

shoes, and really think about this, it makes me shudder.

During my one-hour performance I focused in on Frances, trying my best to offer her a lifeline. My goal, to make her smile and perhaps teach her a thing or two about the benefits of living in that wonderful community. In fact, in the end, it was her who would be teaching me.

At the conclusion of my show, I noticed she opted to stay in the activity room. She sat in her wheelchair, looking out of these beautiful windows overlooking the not so beautiful parking lot. I packed away my last piece of equipment, but before I headed out to my next show, I decided to try one more time to lighten her load. I pulled a nearby folding chair next to her and I began to talk. I asked, "So how do you like it here?" She turned to me instantly, with an almost glare, and responded "I'm the cat."

I was confused, Tom didn't mention anything about dementia, so her absurd response startled me. I thought I would be extra kind and respond to her unusual response with a gentle question, "You're the cat?"

She started; "A couple of years ago, as I sat in my living room, a cat came to my patio door and stared at me for a minute or two and ran away."

I tried to look interested, but I really wanted to look at my watch to see how much time I had to listen to this senile lady. I had to leave soon to get to my next facility. She continued, "Well, that cat did this for a few days in a row, so I decided to open the door to see if she would come in. The next time she appeared, sure enough, she peeked in, stepped through the door for a few seconds and then ran off." I was now zoning out as I tried to manufacture something to say to prove I was listening to this lady's nonsensical story. Even though I really had to get going, she continued. "The next day, I put a bowl of milk down on the floor next to my couch and that cat came all the way into my living room, took a drink and bolted out the door again."

I looked at my watch and prepared my words as to why I had to leave. I just did not have the time to listen to this rambling. Before I could offer my lame excuse, she finished. "The next day, that cat came in again, drank the milk and proceeded to jump up on my couch, curl up and go to sleep."

I was half startled and half confused as I sensed, only by the inflection in her voice, she had just said something important. I re-focused on her face and began once again to really listen to her words, it was just in time to share in the epiphany, as she simply stated…. "I'm the Cat."

239

It hit me like a 2x4 to the side of the head. Frances was teaching me that, just like the cat, she was slowly adjusting to her new surroundings. She was saying she was grateful to be in a secure place where she would be cared for and kept safe. But most of all, she was teaching me that it took a little time to adjust and it could not be rushed. In fact, she was the cat and I was the fool.

I got so caught up in my own abilities in an effort to help, within my timeline, I failed. Frances taught me the lesson that day. The lesson was about dealing with life, loss and and that everyone does it in their own time and in their own way.

"Are You Reelin' in the Years"

That's the question that a Steely Dan song posed way back in 1972, and the answer for me is yes! At 72 years old, I am, in fact, "stowing away the time," as I am slowing down. What actually got me thinking about this was a different song I heard recently called "Old Man," by Neil Young. It actually hit me, pretty hard, right between the eyes. It's a song of a discussion between a young and an old man. The reason I felt the impact so hard was I realized, quite suddenly, that I now identify with the old man in that song instead of the young man.

I don't really know when it happened, but somewhere along the line, I was given a new role by "Father Time," that I did not want, nor ask for. It seems like just yesterday I was the younger man in that song and the sudden switch felt like a gut-punch. It's very similar to the feeling you get when you hear your favorite song has just turned 50 or you see your favorite singer is also getting "long in the tooth."

I'll admit, at first, I was sad, but the incident did open the door to a little self-reflection as this old man started having "the talk" with the young man still dwelling somewhere deep inside me.

Aging gracefully is one of the most difficult tasks we face in our short time here on the planet. There is

241

an old saying "Getting old is not for sissies" and boy, is that right. Doctor and P.T. appointments are only outnumbered by ailments and infirmities. Luckily, our dad taught us kids, by example, how to fight getting old and accepting it when it was time. One of the funniest things he would say to us, until he was almost 90, was "Old age is creepin' in."

He would always work hard at physical labor, reminding us to do the same for as long as we could and, most important, "Never give it away." On the other side of that coin, when it was time for him to give up his keys (and independence) we "kids" fretted over it for weeks. We discussed the plan and practiced our speech, only to be totally shocked with our dad's response on the day of the intervention.

After carefully laying out our case about his failing memory and the dangers of his driving, he simple responded with "Good call" and handed us the keys. He also gave up his house to us kids, long before necessary, just because he felt like it was the right time to do it. What an example he was. I only hope to be as graceful when it's my turn. My music helps me to prepare.

Music has been my life for the last 50 years. It has been my entire career. Lately, many songs have been actual godsends to assist me in the painful process of aging. Music and lyrics have been instrumental

242

in getting me through the myriad of obstacles that getting older keeps throwing at me. There are those songs that help me reminisce like, "In my Life," by the Beatles; "These Days," by Jackson Browne, or "Same Old Lang Syne," by Dan Fogelberg. There are songs that literally instruct me in the process, like James Taylor's "The Secret of Life" and John Denver's "Poems Prayers and Promises." Some songs remind me of the good friends I've made along the way like, "You've Got a Friend" by Carole King or Steve Chapin's "I Let Time Go Lightly."

Lastly there are those poignant songs that can also be hopeful and sad at the same time. The ones on the top of my list are; "It's Your World Now," by the Eagles, and Harry Chapin's "Story of a Life," which reminds me of how lucky I am to have had my wife Denise by my side throughout this entire journey on this long and winding road.

Although I am not retiring just yet, I know I will keep slowing down until my perpetual motion forward comes quietly to a stop. I also know that time is coming, but, in the meantime, I choose to look to my lifelong friend music, to inspire, motivate and re-energize me, as I ask for just one… more… song…(show). A friend of mine once asked, what song I would play, if I knew it was to be the last song I would ever play. The answer is a song that I often play on the quiet ride home after a show. It's a song I would dedicate to all those friends who have supported me along the way and allowed me the privilege of making music my career. It's called, "I'll Play for You," by Seals and Crofts.

There is another song I hear a lot differently today, with these old ears of mine: "Dust in the Wind" by Kansas. I refuse to let that song take up residency in my head, as I am not quite ready to sing auld lang syne…. yet. Instead, I choose to sing, "I've Had the Time of My Life." Yes, old age is creepin' in but……. afterall, "Does anybody really know what time it is?"

Love Live's in a Smile and a Song will always remain in my heart.

Friends & Side by Side

Tony DiGaetano Bill Barlow Joe Trionfero Paul Vandish

244

"Under The Grapevine"
(Together again and forever)

This is the phrase our dad would always use when referring to Heaven. Its origin was his family sitting under the Grapevine on the patio, behind the Trionfero homestead at 36 Herrick Steet. He would assure us, with certainty, that we would all be together again and forever. These are the stories of my faith that are living proof, to me, that Dad was right.

A Man and his Church
St Joseph's was our family's church. This is where we were christened, confirmed and married. Dad planted the seed of faith in all of his kids at a very young age. We were always in our pew every Sunday morning.

245

The Miracle in Johnson City

On March 9th, 2023, I was on the road. It was just like many other days I had, except for one thing. On this day, my dad connected with me, two years after he passed away. I was in Johnson City, New York doing shows at The Susquehanna Nursing Home. Like many other workdays, I had two shows, one at 10 am and one at 2 pm. It was my custom to try to find a quiet spot to park to kill the long break making calls, doing paper work or even getting some sleep.

On that special day in March, I located a Dunkin across from the Oakdale Mall. Normally a Dunkin parking lot would be too busy, but this store front was surrounded by parking lots it shared with other businesses in the area. I drove to the quiet side of this Dunkin where there were no cars and decided to, first, go in for a coffee and a bagel.

(Remember this, as I hit the rewind button to go back in time)

Sometime in the late 1990s my dad and I were working together doing a JTS Music show. YES, my retired father was the oldest "DJ" ever, and he loved it. For whatever reason, we were in his blue van, driving slowly. I was riding shotgun. I don't ever speed, but on that day I "encouraged" my dad to pick it up a bit, as we were running a tad late going to someone's reception to do the music.

I was doing okay until he stopped at a caution light, when he clearly could have made it through. When I mentioned this fact to my dad, he pointed to a tiny piece of white paper taped to his dash. It was The Prayer to St. Gertrude. As he tapped on that paper, he began to teach me a very valuable lesson during the long 30-second delay. He said, "You see this prayer, whenever you're chomping at the bit, say it and you will feel better and make much better use of the time." He continued, "Every time you say that prayer, to St Gertrude, you release a thousand souls from purgatory. "You should learn it."

Needless to say, we made it to the show on time, but after that day I found myself recalling that lesson every time I was stuck in traffic or delayed in some fashion. I finally gave in and, because there was no way I was taping anything to my dash, I memorized the darn thing. I said that prayer thousands of times since. My dad passed in January of 2021 (Covid) and that prayer meant even more to me. Turns out, it meant even more to him than I thought, as when we were dismantling his home, we found that same prayer taped his wall. At his wake, my sister even had copies of it as a prayer card to give to his grandkids.

(Now back to March 9 2023)

As I stepped out of my vehicle to head to the Dunkin door, on the other side of the building, two things happened. I noticed the beautiful view of the countryside and also, in the middle of that beautiful view, was a Dunkin sign that read, Help Wanted. I chuckled to myself as I thought how our dad would find both of those things equally beautiful. He would have loved that "panoramic view," and he would have loved that job too.

Literally, the moment I finished that thought I noticed "something shiny" on the otherwise grey, dull pavement. In the middle of nowhere, in the middle of a giant empty parking lot, at that precise moment, sat a prayer card. It had the face of Jesus on it. As I reached down to pick up that card, I thought, possibly, my dad was reaching out to me. When I turned the card over, I became sure. Right in front of me, on the back of that card, was The Prayer to St Gertrude. There were no calculable odds that I would have found that prayer card, in that spot at that time. I teared up and called my sister to tell her of this amazing event. Dad had called.

It was a miracle, plain and simple. It was so comforting and reassuring knowing our dad was in heaven and still looking out for us. Just as he had done so many times before. Reminding his kids not to be sad, we would all be together again and forever.

In case you haven't gathered, yet, I am a man of strong faith who absolutely believes in miracles. I truly believe that IF WE LISTEN hard enough, God, and those we love, will talk to us.

Afterall, God is love and; "Love Lives in a Smile."

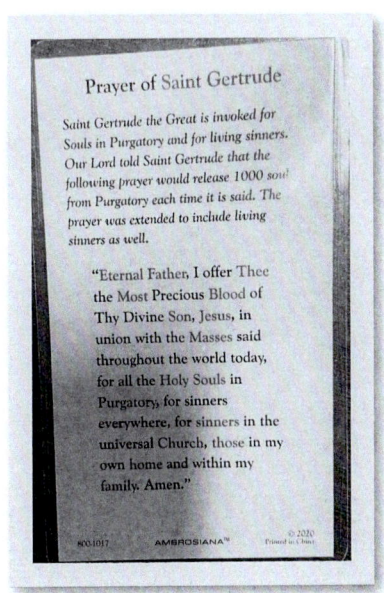

The Words in Red

Somewhere around the turn of the century I became extremely frustrated with the planet Earth. Actually, my problem was with the humans that inhabited it. I was closing in on fifty years old and I felt lost and floundering as I saw civilization, in general, beginning to be decay exponentially. There was so much selflessness and hypocrisy. We absolutely were living in scary times and I had grandkids.

I was lost, I did not know where to turn or who to follow. I knew there had to be more to life than what I was witnessing around me. I used to trust the news to guide me, but the days of Walter Cronkite were long gone. As much as I loved my music, I found my favorites being drowned out by the new billion-dollar pop stars. Even sports became commercialized and lost to me. Even though I loved Derek Jeter, he wouldn't be my savior nor the solution to my discontent.

I needed a leader, someone to follow. I abandoned politics and the hope that any politician (or party) was going to lead me to the promised land. I needed more than a new direction, I needed someone I could trust with my life, but more importantly, my soul. Enter Jesus.

Having a strong foundation of faith that, thank God, my parents were wise enough to instill in me as a child, I had my answer. I would turn to Jesus and He would be my new guide and the Bible would be my new road map. Did I mention that I am an impatient, impetuous, hyper active person with a dash of OCD? One of my favorite sayings is, "God give me patience and I want it now." This sums me up pretty well. At first, my plan was to read the Bible, but after a chapter or two (okay a half of chapter), I decided I really only wanted to know what Jesus said; after all, I knew He was my chosen leader and I was in a hurry.

That's when I had my epiphany. I remembered a bible my Aunt Rosie and Uncle Carmen (my Godparents) had given me as a kid. I somehow recalled that any time Jesus talked/taught, THE WORDS WERE IN RED. I had my answer. I only needed to focus on the four Gospels and those words in red. Well, after a few times of reading those gospels, I realized I still struggled to stay focused and engaged. It got complicated.

Then God gave me the answer and I found it on the New York State Thruway. My chosen career took me on the road a lot. In fact, I have driven over a million miles in my quest to teach the message of Christ in my program called "The Show of Love."

251

So, I had the time to actually start listening to those 4 gospels while driving. Instead of listening to (bad) news, music or books on tape I could discover the meaning of life and the pathway to eternal peace. Talk about your win-win, I hit the JACKPOT!

This started an 11-year journey of me listening to nothing else but those four books of, Mathew, Mark, Luke and John on CD's. Rather than relying on others to explain to me what Jesus said, or meant, I listened and decided for myself what those words in red really meant. My goal was not memorization of chapter and verse, but to capture the essence of Christ message.

After a couple of years, I compiled a list of Jesus' top ten lessons:
Have Faith, Show Mercy, Be Humble, Forgive, Don't Worry, Don't Judge, Don't Sin. Love God and each other, Serve God and not money, and Spread the Word of the Lord, AMEN! I memorized these and recited them to my grandkids many times. One of my proudest moments ever, came as I was raking leaves one day with a few of them and my grandson Joseph recited these to me, unsolicited.

As we all know, the world hasn't gotten any better and, instead, a climate of hatred, indifference and selflessness crept over the entire planet. My mission became more urgent and I needed to pick up the pace and stream line His/my message. I decided to just focus on the main message of Jesus. What was it's (His) essence? After much reflection and even more consolidation, I came up with a new list of the top 10 lessons of Christ. Specifically teaching us how we should treat one another, what did Jesus actually say about human interaction:

Love They Neighbor, Love Your Enemy, Love One Another, Forgive One Another, Do unto Others Has You Would Have Others Do unto You, Do Not Judge, Let He with No Sin Cast The 1st Stone, Turn the Other Cheek, I Desire Mercy not Sacrifice and Forgive Us Our Trespasses as We Forgive Those That Trespass Against Us.

There is a pretty obvious theme here but these are not easy lessons.

These Christian tenants certainly don't come natural to us mere mortals. Turns out, I am a sinner too. What is a parent or grandparent to do to save this planet and the people they share it with? I did one more consolidation and it hangs on a yellow Post It note on my wall. It all comes down to this, when considering how we should treat others;

Help, Don't Hurt, Be Kind, Forgive, Don't Judge.

You know what, it turns out I didn't even need any list after all. I knew the answer as a 6-year-old, (after my 1st Communion.) We all know the answer, "Treat People the Way You Want to Be Treated."

Jesus did say "The new command is this: Love One Another."

The most important thing we can do for our children and grandchildren is to teach them that same lesson that we learned and lead by example.

HEIP
Don't Hurt
Be KinD
forgive
Don't Judge

Miracle at the Corner of 1st and Bridge

On the evening of Friday Nov. 28, 1975, at precisely 6:00 PM, Gary Ingersoll, of the Oswego Jaycees, was sealed into the phone booth on the corner of West 1st and Bridge by the police chief Robert LaTulip. He would remain in that confined space for a duration of 24 hours. His goals:

1. Set the world's record for being locked into an outdoor phone booth (24 hours straight)
2. Raise money for some deserving kids of Oswego, NY.

On the Friday after Thanksgiving, (before it was called black Friday) the Oswego Jaycees (and their counterparts the Jayncees) had a goal of raising $200 to take 40 kids shopping for Christmas. It was called, "Project Christmas Call." The fine people of Oswego could call that phone booth number and pledge a donation for the kids. Gary was sealed into that box for what would be a 25-hour marathon, including a cold November night in the port city on the lake.

Gary couldn't leave for anything. (Yes, he was given a bucket to help answer when nature called.) What happened on that late fall night in Oswego was only the first of two miracles. On the long cold night, where the temperature actually dipped into the 20s, the phone, in that booth, rang all night

255

long. People called in to donate and speak to the "Jaycee Wise Man."

Over $800 in small donations was collected. This was a lot of money for 1975. It was all from just ordinary, wonderful citizens of our Port City. What started out as a goal of helping 40 kids ended up helping 200 kids and pushing the Christmas Spirit into the stratosphere.

On December 10th, just 12 days later, an army of Jaycees and Jayncees ended up taking these 200 kids on a Christmas shopping spree at the Grants Department store in the plaza on Route 104 East. This is where the second miracle happened.

It was an evening that none of us would ever forget. There were isles of toys prepared for the kids to shop in, but what happened next took us all by surprise. God was in the house that night as something happened that none of us saw coming.

The 200 children were broken up into groups of five or so with an adult supervisor leading the way. In every single one of those separate groups, one kid after another would ask if they could spend their money on gifts for others. They thought of, and bought for, their parents and siblings instead of themselves.

It was inexplicable and the adults in the room were given a lesson in the true meaning of Christmas. Tom Price says, "There were lots of happy tears in the store that night."

Yes, Gary Ingersall was the hero that night, (sadly, we lost him at a very young age,) but there were many other men and women of the Oswego Jaycees who helped make this happen. The project itself was the brainchild of four really good friends. Co-Chairs Tom Price, Frank Krul, Gary Ingersoll and myself. The amazing committee also consisted of Mike Davis, Michael Coad and Bill Young (RIP). They were the ones who also stood outside that long cold night with Gary. They were the ones encouraging him, feeding him, handing him THE bucket. They also were the ones holding the curtain around the booth to give Gary his privacy when needed.

On the night of the shopping spree, there were many helpers. Mike Shrader, Marshall & Jeanne Trionfero, Dave Murray, Charlie Durante, Jim & Chris Bushy, Dan & Adele Brown, Liz Price, Rosemary Batista, Irene Krul, & Joanne Palmitese.

The real heroes of that nights were the givers. First, the callers who graciously gave to the kids and to those same kids who lovingly passed them on to their families. It was truly the miracle at the corner of 1st and Bridge.

On November 28, 1975, the emphasis was, in fact, more on the White Christmas than the Black Friday!

And Who Is My Neighbor......

I am a 72-year-old man from Oswego, NY, who is a husband, father of five and a grampa of eleven. I am also a professional entertainer who has performed my entire life. Most of all, I am the "Show of Love Guy." (That's what the kids call me.) For the past 36 years, I have worked as an undercover agent for Jesus, disguised as a motivational speaker doing school assembly programs.

Having performed my shows at schools over 4300 times during the past three dozen years, I have actually encouraged over a million students to follow the message of Christ: "Love Thy Neighbor as Thyself." I do modify His message into something they better understand, a phrase they've heard since they were little children; "Treat People the Way You Want to Be Treated." This is who I am. I am not a Democrat or a Republican, nor am I an imposter. I am a follower of Christ. I am a Christian.

And who is my neighbor? This was actually the second (and more important) question posed to Jesus by an expert in the law in the parable of the Good Samaritan. (Luke 10 25-37) It is paramount to remember that the first question asked of Jesus by the scribe was, "What must I do to inherit eternal life?"

One might think that this would be the most important question of all time. However, once it's agreed upon that in order to get into Heaven you must "Love thy neighbor as thyself," the expert in the law, "wanting to justify himself," asks that fateful second question, "And who is my neighbor?" Even though Jesus told us what to do to gain eternal life, He goes one step further and shows us how to do it…. And that's the ticket.

Jesus describes who our neighbor is in the parable. In answering this question, Jesus tells a story of a man being attacked by robbers on the dangerous road between Jerusalem and Jericho. Christ tells of a Priest and a Levite (both upright men) who, upon seeing the victim in distress, cross over to the other side and abandon the man in need.

In stunning contrast, and in a purposeful manner, Jesus tells us it is a Samaritan, who is the one that stops and shows mercy by helping the fallen man. His choice of Samaritan is not random, it is monumental, since, at the time, they were hated due to their ethnicity, religion or social standing. When Jesus asks, "Which of these three do you think was a neighbor to the man who fell into the hands of robbers?" the expert of the law admits it was "The one who had mercy."

And why does this matter? With this parable, Jesus is giving us the ultimate Christian teaching that is so important in our world today. The same world in which we are all so concerned about, because of our kids and grandkids. It's this lesson he taught on several occasions in the Gospels. The most important "law," that will lead us to eternal peace is "To Love God" and "To love one another." He stresses to "Love thy neighbor as ourselves." We are all equal in God's eyes, we are all God's children and we are all loved by him. When Jesus says "Love thy neighbors, he means to love ALL of our neighbors.

THERE ARE NO EXCEPTIONS TO HIS GOLDEN RULE.

Regardless of our ethnicity, religion or social standing, no matter what our differences are, we must love one another!

I was shown how to be a good Christian by my parents, Joe & Inez Trionfero. They both modeled Christ-like behavior with every encounter they had with family, friends or strangers.

On September 5th 2025, at one of my last Show of Love assemblies at Kingsford Park, a Young 5th grader was called to the stage. Her name was Imagine. She reminded me, once again, of God's plan and my purpose. It was she, and hundreds of participants like her, who motivated me. If you have followed any of my many stories, you will notice they are peppered with the goodness that I have learned from all of my interactions with these innocent and beautiful kids. As Jesus said, "To enter the kingdom of Heaven one must change and become like the little children." I have learned so much from them.

It's the kids who can teach us:
1. "This land is your land, this land is my land"
2. "With Liberty and justice **FOR ALL**"
3. "What the World Needs Now is Love Sweet Love"
4. "Treat People the Way You Want to Be Treated"
   (NO EXCEPTIONS)

Our children have shown us how to do it. Now it's up to us. As Jesus said at the end of that Good Samaritan Parable: **"Go and Do Likewise."**

God is Love and "Love Lives in a Smile"
Joe Trionfero

The Three Folding Chairs

On January 30th, 2009, on one of my many trips to do a show at Trinity Catholic School (St. Paul's) in Oswego, NY, something very unusual happened. It was during "Catholic Schools Week." I was setting up folding chairs for the assembly program in the school gym, which would be held at 2:00 PM, and some 5th grade boys had "volunteered" to help me set up the chairs for the teachers and guest. I was pulling chairs from stacks against the wall and turning to hand them off to a student, just like in a makeshift water brigade line.

At precisely 1:40 PM (I have the time stamp from the photo) I turned and handed three 3 folding chairs to the kid behind me and reached back to the stack to grab three more. As I reached back again to hand them off..... the previous three chairs were still there, STANDING ALONE. The boy had got distracted (surprise) and we all just stood there staring at those three chairs. We all waited with anticipation for them to fall. They did not. We probably would have stood there much longer but the show started in about fifteen minutes so we had to disturb the chairs ourselves and continue to set up. Before we grabbed those chairs, I did take the picture.

The kids did think it was kind of cool, but in my silly mind I was thinking, miracle? You see, over my last fifty years of doing assembly programs, I have had the opportunity to handle a few folding chairs. It had never happened before and it has never happened since, despite my efforts.

The boys and I even tried several times at the end of that show to replicate the event. We could not. I'm just saying it was unusual, to say the least, that three folding chairs at Trinity Catholic stood alone. I did point this out to the Principal David Friedlander at the time and he was pretty amazed as well. I am sure most people would call my three folding chairs a coincidence, but there are a few of us who would call it more. A friend of mine once told me that "A coincidence was God's way of wishing to remain anonymous." Maybe it was God's hand holding up those chairs or it could have just been a stroke of luck. I choose to BELIEVE he had a hand in it. I am absolutely certain that if we truly listen, God will speak to us. Will we hear him?

Late Birthday Wish

I turned 72 in mid-August. As I was blowing out the candles on my cake, I forgot to make my wish. Instead, I was distracted by a fleeting thought. Just for a moment, I allowed myself to consider the imaginary battery icon just over my right shoulder, similar to the one on my phone. I realized, based on the average life expectancy of a male in the United States, my remaining charge was at about 7%. This stung a bit, as it naturally propelled my thoughts to the impending eternity and the state of the world I would be leaving behind for my grandkids. In 2008, Kenny Chesney did a song with a poignant message; "Everybody wants to go to Heaven but nobody wants to go today."

I have understood, for quite some time now, that life is unfair, fragile and, at best…. fast. At this particular moment, as the smoke rose from my cake towards the ceiling, I had a disconcerting feeling, as I felt "Forever" staring me down at my own kitchen table and in front of my beautiful family. Once again, I thank God in Heaven and for Heaven, as He saved me again from sliding down that proverbial rabbit hole of facing my own mortality. I, once again, relied on my faith to save me from the dark cloud gathering in my mind and above my kitchen table.

Thanks to my parents, Joe and Inez Trionfero, I have a shield against death. I am a Christian. I was raised to be a follower of Christ. From the moment I was old enough to remember, my entire childhood seemed to be centered around our dad making sure that our butts were in our pew at St. Joseph's Church every Sunday morning. This is where we learned about the teachings of Jesus. Just as important, our parents modeled the Christ-like virtues that we learned from that altar on West 1st Street in Oswego. Our faith and our God were at the very core of everything we did as a family.

There is a slight problem. Although, I know, with every fiber of my being, that being a faithful follower of Jesus will be my ticket to get into Heaven, I am a sinful man. I have to be honest, there are indeed moments that I am painfully aware that I am only human. A lot like Peter, I question whether or not I am still a worthy follower. I have had my failures in life and my lapses in faith. God knows I have made mistakes! After a lifetime of these "slip-ups," I do sometimes worry and wonder and have doubts that begin to consume me.

It's when the Grim Reaper starts closing in on me that I always, instinctually, run back to the teachings of Christ to protect me. I begin to refocus and look for that sure-fire ticket to get me admission to beyond those pearly gates. The most predominate

267

thought of my life, lately, has been the desire to get to Heaven and spend all of eternity with my God, my parents and all of those that I love and miss so much. So, at these times of uncertainty, I often revert back to the four Gospels scouring for hidden clues or secrets buried within those pages to guarantee my all-access pass.

I have spent years being a novice student of the tenets of Christianity looking for that silver bullet that would offer me both internal and eternal peace. Maybe it was because, this time, I was looking through 72-year-old eyes or perhaps it because of my growing, deep concern that my grandkids' world is going to hell. I am not sure why, but I did have an unusual revelation.

The answer has always been right before my eyes. There, on those pages in those four books (Mathew, Mark, Luke and John) were many passages where Jesus is asked, point blank, what must one do to gain eternal life? In other words, what's the winning ticket that will gain me entry into the promised land? Jesus simply states, on multiple occasions, that all one must do to, "inherit eternal life" is to, "Love God and to love our neighbor as ourselves." Whew, I thought… I can do that.

The fact of the matter is I am well aware that the Devil has been working overtime to dishearten me with the news of the day and my impending departure. So, I have already been working on this "Love one another thing." My goal is to make this world a better place and afford my grandkids the same wonderful experience I have had while on this planet.

I have been doing my best to show love and spread this message of Christ. I battle the devil daily. Instead of taking the bait, and being mad, sad or scared about death and the uncertain world we live in…. I choose Love. It's the only thing that will conquer hate. It is also the absolute best thing I can do to lead my tribe (29 of us) into Heaven so we can all be together forever.

So, if it's not too late… I would like to make my birthday wish now. It would not be for a quick charge to extend my battery life. My wish would simply be for me to use whatever time, talents and treasure I have left to convince my family to follow me (and Jesus) to Heaven.

Remember, God is Love. Love is the Answer. "Love Lives in a Smile." ☺

AMOR TRIONFERA

"LOVE WILL TRIUMPH"